A Taste of Madras

A SOUTH INDIAN COOKBOOK

A Taste of
Madras

A SOUTH INDIAN COOKBOOK

RANI KINGMAN

INTERLINK BOOKS

An imprint of Interlink Publishing Group, Inc.

NEW YORK

First American edition published 1996 by
INTERLINK BOOKS
An imprint of Interlink Publishing Group, Inc.
99 Seventh Avenue • Brooklyn, New York 11215

Originally published in Great Britain by Garnet Publishing Limited

Library of Congress Cataloging-in-Publication Data

Kingman, Rani.
    A taste of Madras : a South Indian cookbook / Rani Kingman.
        p.   cm.
    Includes index.
    ISBN 1-56656-195-7 (hbk.) — ISBN 1-56656-196-5 (pbk.)
    1. Cookery, Indic—Southern style.   2. Cookery—India—Tamil Nadu.
I. Title.
TX724.5.I4K56   1966
641.5954'8—dc20   95-49065
                                               CIP

Project management, editing: Jackie Jones
Design: Christine Wood
Food photography: James Duncan
Stylist: Madeleine Brehaut
Food preparation for photography: Sue Maggs
Location photographs kindly supplied by Danny Brannigan
Editing and proofreading: Eileen Cadman, Michèle Clarke,
Ruth Lane Moushabeck, Tim Watson, Jenny Kilgore
Index: Hilary Bird
Production: Sarah Golden
Reprographics: CCTS Ltd, London

Printed and bound in Hong Kong

10   9   8   7   6   5   4   3   2   1

CONTENTS

PREFACE 7

MADRAS 8

RICE 12

BREADS AND PANCAKES 26

VEGETABLES 40

FISH AND SEAFOOD 64

MEAT AND POULTRY 86

CHUTNEYS, PICKLES, RELISHES 114

TIFFIN:
SAVORIES 125
SWEETS AND DESSERTS 139
DRINKS 150

GLOSSARY OF INGREDIENTS 153

WHERE TO FIND INGREDIENTS 158

INDEX 159

Unestranged kinship breeds unabating wealth.

THE "TIRRUKARAL"

To my mother, Mrs. Anne Rebecca Arumainayagam, née Rungaswamy
to my sons Billy and Raji Kingman
and to the memory of my grandmothers and my mother-in-law: Mrs. Ponnamal Arumainayagam,
née Devanayagam; Mrs. Charlotte Elizabeth Rungaswamy, née Vedanayagam;
Mrs. Maud Elsie Kingman, née Harley.

ACKNOWLEDGMENTS

*Neither earth or heaven can truly repay spontaneous aid . . . help given regardless of return is
wider than the sea.*

The verses above, taken from the ancient poem the "Tirrukaral" express my thanks to those who have made this book possible. My husband, Bob Kingman, gave me a lot of understanding, encouragement and help for which I am grateful. I would like to thank my mother, who prepared and showed me all the tempting dishes, and my father who inspired and encouraged me to write them down. To my grandmothers and aunts who passed on to me some of the old family recipes and allowed me to share them I owe my gratitude. Thank you Rachel, Carole, John, Maureen and David (my sisters, sister-in-law and brothers), Margery Harley, Geraldine and Tony Montalbano, who gave me a home to stay in on my visits to London and shared some of their ideas with me. Billy and Raji, my sons, my nephews Anthony and Jamie and niece Francesca tried whatever I prepared without too much complaint.

I had help with the typing of my manuscript from my friends Jane McKee, Pat Hirst, Elizabeth Bennett and Robin Bennett and I am grateful to them for their time and effort. Mary Gibson and Laura Gillespy were willing victims who have tried some of my dishes. Many thanks to Danny Brannigan for his photographs. To my other friends who listened and helped me in little ways, thank you.

I would like to thank Clarissa Dickson-Wright, who encouraged and helped me to find a publisher. My gratitude and thanks to my editors Jackie Jones and Eileen Cadman who gave me their expertise, hard work and support and got the best out of my manuscript, and gave me a chance to share what I have learned about Tamilian cuisine and culture.

Nandri. Thank you.

Preface

As a young girl growing up in Madras I learned many customs regarding food as I watched my mother at work in her kitchen. Later, I learned to cook as my grandmother, my mother and my aunts all showed me their recipes and their techniques. Now I have written down the recipes passed down to me, so that my sons – who have grown up with the richness of two cultures – and others may learn the traditions of Madras.

For Tamilians, food is closely connected with many customs and beliefs, all of which formed an inherent part of my upbringing. So alongside my recipes I have tried to convey a little of the philosophy that underlies this cuisine, as well as the day-to-day practices associated with foods and cooking.

The kitchen in a Tamilian home, where the preparation and cooking begins, is considered pure and sacred. The cook, who has to wash thoroughly before she starts preparing the meals and may not be touched while cooking, is not permitted to taste any of the food during the course of preparation because it may become polluted. So Tamilian cooks learn to measure by sight, and to gauge the flavor from the cooking aromas. Consequently, in writing down my recipes, it has not always been easy to give precise quantities for this ingredient or that, nor precise cooking times – however, all the recipes have been carefully recorded and tested, and they taste just as they should.

I hope you enjoy learning about these beliefs and customs from Madras, which I am proud of, and that the taste of Madras gives your kitchen a Tamilian warmth and hospitality.

The first virtue in any creed is to share your food and cherish all life.
From the "Tirrukaral"

7

MADRAS

Madras lies along the Malabar and Coromandel coasts of South India, washed by three seas. I use the name as it was used in the past, meaning the state of Tamil Nadu, rather than the city alone. Madras is a land of surf, spice and magic, a land of temples with a profusion of orange flowers, shade of the banyan tree, the *minqu* drum, chime of the bell, the heady scents of incense and spices. Out in the Bay of Bengal lie the paradise archipelagoes of the Andaman and Nicobar islands, where the crystal-clear waters shimmer with tropical fish amongst the coral. Many Tamilians look to the sea for their livelihood: seafood, rich in variety, and plentiful, has given rise to a range of delicious seafood dishes. Inland, Madras is largely agricultural – its warm temperatures, fertile soil and rainfall permitting good crops. Coconut and tamarind are two of the crops that characterize the region's food. Rice is a staple (though it, and sugar, are rationed in order that sufficient quantities can be exported as cash-earners). Peanuts, mustard and sesame are grown, and inland the more temperate hills are the home of tea and coffee plantations.

A BRIEF HISTORY

The sea has always been greatly important for the Tamilians, as a source of food and as a highway for voyages east and west. We know that as early as the 6th century BC ships from southeast India voyaged to the Malay peninsula and Burma in search of precious metals – and by the 1st century AD there was extensive traffic and trading across the Indian Ocean, acquiring spices and other goods from Southeast Asia (traded in India and taken westward to Europe by merchants from Greece and Rome).

Madurai (capital of the Pandyan kingdom) acquired great wealth, as it was the crossroads of trading routes that brought all manner of items from every part of India to the south, where they were traded with merchants from Rome and elsewhere. Pepper, "black gold," was grown on the Malabar and Coromandel coasts, and was used as a medium of trade. St. Thomas the Apostle came to Kerala (to the west of Madras) in 52AD, and is said to have been martyred near the present-day city of Madras around 70AD, since when the Christian faith has survived in Madras. (At around the same time, a Jewish community was founded in Cochin – also in Kerala.) Close contact between India and Southeast Asia persisted for over a thousand years – and around the 11th century the great Tamil empire of the Cholas dominated Southeast Asia as well as a huge expanse of south India. The powerful Hindu empires prevented the south of India undergoing Muslim invasions on the scale of those in the north.

The next significant impact came from the British, initially via the East India Company – in fact, the land of the city was leased by the Company and a trading port established (1640). The British sold Indian produce (silks and cottons, indigo dye and opium) to China, in exchange for China tea. The town of Pondicherry was a French trading post, and from time to time the French and British would fight out their European battles on Indian soil. In time, of course, Madras became part of the Raj, with its influences and legacy.

OF FOOD AND PHILOSOPHY IN MADRAS

Though the Tamilians have their own distinct history and characteristics, something all Indians have in common is the ancient custom of hospitality. Indian hospitality is teamed with excellent food and gracious service and has to be experienced – for it is like no other in the world.

Food is traditionally served on platters with raised edges, called *thal* for men and *thali* for the smaller version used by women. These trays were once made of brass, copper and silver, though now they are usually stainless steel. Individual dishes are then served in *katora* or *katori*, which keep the dishes separate so the individual can enjoy the aromas and flavors of each dish. The traditional serving vessels – of vivid enameled metals, of porcelain or metals engraved and chased, of brass on steel, and gold on silver – were the focal point of display; they have now been replaced by stainless-steel dishes wrapped in gaily colored cloths of cotton and silk. When food is served the cloths are folded back loosely around the container.

To eat, people sit on woven mats, while the richer Tamilians sit on *jamakalams,* or cotton sheets of many colors that were hand-blocked in the old days. My English dinner table is laid with Indian cloths of brilliant red, lapis lazuli and magenta, for I love these strong colors.

Sweetmeats, symbols of welcome, love and hospitality, may be eaten at almost any time of the day, and are always offered to guests. Hospitality is important to Tamilians and to insult a host's hospitality – however unwittingly – is unforgivable. Guests should take a little of whatever is put before them, and if it is not to their taste the remainder may be left on the plate.

Savories and sweets are inevitably linked together, as are all things in Tamilians' lives, as they believe life to be a circle. We are born, we live and die, and are reborn. Foods that have warmth should always be coupled with those that have a quality of coolness – this tradition goes back two thousand years in our culture.

The daily life of the Hindu is affected by the elements of sky, air, water, fire and earth and the times of the day: dawn, morning, afternoon, evening, dusk and night. The elements play an important part in food: certain spices produce heat in the body, such as chili and pepper. Limes and other citrus fruits are considered cooling. Certain meat is supposed to produce heat. Fish and vegetables are regarded as cooling, though crab and shrimp are considered bad in excess. A cold food may also be thought to have warmth in it – strangely enough, ice is considered warming, as is *kulfi* (ice cream)! When I was a college student in Madras, I was discouraged from eating citrus fruits during the monsoon season as they were too cooling. The correct balance has to be achieved, and this is the responsibility of the cook.

Water, one of the elements in Hindu astrology, affects the life and diet of the Tamilian. Water symbolizes blood, and Indian philosophers consider it very important. A bath is important before the start of the day, and if there is a river nearby people will even take a dip to be cleansed. Seafood, living in the water, is eaten to keep a balance in the body at all times.

Many Tamilians' homes have wells in the backyard. Water in the well is used for cleaning, bathing and washing dishes. Water for cooking and drinking is collected from pumps and usually carried to the houses by women, in clay pots carried on their heads. Drinking water is boiled, then cooled and kept in clay pots, while water for cooking is kept in big stainless-steel and brass pots. They are all stored separately. Rose essence is mixed in water and sprinkled by young maidens over guests at weddings, as a blessing. Every three years, pilgrims who can, go to the Ganges to be blessed and cleaned in its holy waters. In August, celebrations are held to mark the birth of the god Ganesh, and culminate in small Ganesh models being thrown into the water. And Christians (the second largest group in Madras) are baptized in water by priests.

Purity is important to Tamilians, especially in connection with food, and we observe this in a number of ways: shoes may not be worn in the house, where people sit, eat and sleep on the floor; clothes worn outside, for whatever activity, are changed before eating; the right hand only is used for eating (after thorough washing); each plate is served individually and individual little bowls for extra fare are placed on the table; when Tamilians drink they lift the cup and drink from it without touching it with their lips; water in a stainless-steel pitcher and a tumbler for the water are the only items on the table before the meal; it is considered unhygienic for the food to be laid out, as it may become contaminated; each family member has his own thali and tumbler, and it would be considered impure to share them with others; the plates used by guests may be used only once, so to avoid waste fresh banana leaves are used, clean and pure themselves.

Vegetarianism in Madras

It is often thought that all south Indians are vegetarians, but this isn't so. Though strict Hindus (particularly the Brahmin caste) eat no meat or fish, most other Hindus do eat meat if they can afford it – though not beef, as the cow is considered sacred. Muslims in Madras, of course, eat no pork. Lamb is popular (though often very expensive nowadays) as is goat (especially kid) and chicken (in practice, both beef and pork are on sale in the city, and are easily available in the countryside where people keep their own animals). However, when meat is eaten it is generally in very small quantities: usually just one meat or fish dish is served along with three or four vegetable dishes, plus rice or bread. It is quite normal for everybody to eat vegetarian meals on some days, and there is a high level of understanding about the restrictions on other people's diets.

Spices, aromatics and cooking techniques

Tamilian cookery has a system of its own, albeit unwritten. The knowledge and skills have been handed down from mother to daughter by word of mouth and by practical example.

The right mixture and balance of flavors and textures is the essence of good Tamilian cooking. However, flavor and taste have always been personal, so feel free to make slight changes in the quantity of spices and choice of meat, fish or vegetables in the recipes in this book. Bear in mind, however, that halving or doubling the quantity of ingredients could alter the consistency of the dishes.

Like other Indians, Tamilians use no curry powders – even the well known *garam masala* is not used in Tamilian cooking. The main spices used are chili, turmeric, coriander and cumin. Salt is the most important of all seasonings and Tamilians use the zesty pungent rock salt available in India, which is sometime just called "rock." Sugar, honey and raisins are considered sweet seasonings in many dishes. Citrus juices, other juices and tamarind act as acidic seasonings. Fresh, delicate-flavored coriander leaves (cilantro), sweet *neem* leaves (with their intriguing aroma that hints of truffle) and mint – which needs no introduction – are a few of the herbs used in Tamilian dishes. Tamilians are leisure-loving people and in the hot afternoons things slow down – this is reflected in the long hours in which foods are marinated. Spices, giving sweet and sharp flavorings when combined with citrus juices or yogurt, help tenderize and aromatize food.

Onions, shallots, garlic, ginger and fresh chilies are known as aromatics. They are prominent in Tamilian cooking as they give flavor and body to the various dishes. Juices from meat or vegetables, together with ground aromatics and spices, provide the thickening in Tamilian dishes. Sauces may vary in color from light gold to dark gold and dark red, depending on how well the onions are browned and how much chili powder and turmeric are used. The timing of seasoning is important, and salt is best added after the aromatics and meat are browned, as it will otherwise spoil the dry sauté.

Many dishes are cooked by a method of sautéing then steaming – vegetables are cut into small pieces and added to sautéed aromatics along with salt and very little water. They are then covered with a tightly fitting lid and cooked over a high heat, which is then reduced. The steam in the pan should be sufficient to cook the food. Other foods are deep fried – properly deep-fried food is crisp, light and truly clean in taste and appearance. Sometimes food is simply sautéed in ghee, a method especially good for thinnish fillets of best-quality meat. Garnishing and decoration of food is kept simple: a sprinkling of freshly chopped green herbs or of nuts such as cashews or almonds suffices.

A NOTE ON QUANTITIES

Most of these recipes serve four, assuming that about four dishes, plus rice or breads, are served.

RICE

The rich and fertile plains of the Cauvery (in the center of Tamil Nadu), the Ponnayar, Palan, Vargai and Coovum rivers are extensively cultivated with many varieties of rice, and the goddess of the monsoon, Parvati, is highly venerated so that there will be a good rice harvest each year.

One of the most popular (and expensive) long-grain varieties is called *ponni*, used for a wide range of dishes. This is my favorite rice: it is named after the heroine of a Tamil myth, and Ponni is one of my names. (Ponni is used in Tamil Nadu rather than *patna*, which is not grown there, but in some recipes I have specified patna rice, as ponni is difficult to obtain in the West.) Other more basic and commonly used varieties are "black" (not the same as black grains of wild rice) and "glutinous" rice, both of which are used for puddings. Basmati rice – the "queen" of rices – is used only on very special occasions such as weddings and religious festivals, and is an extremely important and valuable commodity.

Tamil Nadu is self-sufficient in rice, partly because of the fertility of the soil, and long traditions of water conservation schemes and management, but partly thanks to government funding of water conservation and well management. In 1976, because rice was being removed from Tamil Nadu for sale in other states, police barriers were set up at the borders to stop the smuggling. It was causing shortages and encouraging black market sales, especially of the more valuable rices such as basmati.

Whereas people in northern India supplement rice with bread in the form of *chappatis* and *pooris*, rice is the main staple in the south and is eaten twice a day by the average family, usually with a sauce to make it more interesting. Among the favorite sauces are *sambar* (a deliciously spiced lentil and vegetable sauce, quite thin in texture), *rassam* or pepperwater (often drunk at the end of the meal), *devanayagam puli kolomba* (a sauce of eggplant and tamarind, which goes extremely well with fried fish too) and simple yogurt (see the section on chutneys for recipes).

Rice is used in both savory and sweet dishes, and is combined with *ulandu* (flour made from black grams, *urad dhall*) to make breakfast dishes such as *idlis, dosais* and *appams* (see Breads and Pancakes). No religious festival is complete without rice. One of the most important of these is Pongal, a harvest festival celebrated in January – and one of the rice desserts in the Tiffin section is named after it.

Rice is considered too important for any of it to be wasted – any leftover rice is washed then dried in the sun. Later it is deep-fried and served as an accompaniment. The starchy cooking water is sometimes saved, then drunk when cool.

The very first cooking lesson a Tamil girl is given by her mother is how to boil the rice. This is seen as important because, when she marries, a Tamil husband appreciates and judges her skills as a cook from the first time she serves it. A frequent topic of conversation at a dinner party is how to cook rice well, and the pitfalls each person has fallen into before being able to cook basmati or patna or ponni correctly!

The electric rice cooker has been a time-saving gift to those modern Tamil women who work outside the home, but in the rural villages women still use the method passed down from their mothers – and although these methods may be simple, there is still an art to them.

First I describe the basic method, then I give some simple variations of it. You can use these versatile recipes at any time with any dish, according to preference. The ingredients for all of them are easily available and each has its own texture and distinctive character. Variety is the spice of life in Madras!

COOKING RICE

Since the basic art of cooking rice is so important, it is appropriate to begin this section with one of the most simple methods, taught to me by my mother. It requires no special effort and any reasonable pan may be used. (In India, rice cooked by this method is boiled in a small rounded pot, with a lid that has holes in it to drain the starch at the end of cooking. At home I use a saucepan with a heavy base – to prevent sticking or burning – with a lid with a special vent in it to drain any excess water.)

Rice and its cooking water should always be measured by volume, not weight – the proportions are important so it is essential to measure both rice and water carefully. Different types of rice will require slightly different cooking times, depending on their size and moisture content – experiment a little until you have it exactly right for your favorite rice.

Simple rice

SATHAM

2 cups water

1 cup long-grain white rice

salt to taste

1. Bring the water to the boil in a heavy-based saucepan.

2. Meanwhile wash the rice thoroughly and leave to drain.

3. When water boils add the washed rice and salt to taste and cover the saucepan.

4. Lower the heat and cook the rice for 10 minutes – check to see whether it is cooked. If not, replace the lid and return to the heat for another 3–5 minutes, until cooked. If there is any remaining water drain it, give the saucepan a shake before putting it back over the heat for a few seconds. The rice is ready to serve.

VARIATIONS

Buttered rice

VENNAI SATHAM

2 cups water

1 cup long-grain white rice

salt to taste

2 tablespoons melted butter or ghee

In this recipe, the butter or ghee adds a little richness and helps to separate the grains.

1. Prepare the rice as stated in the recipe for simple rice, above.

2. Add the butter or ghee just before the end of cooking. (This rice can be kept warm, covered, until required.)

Decorated rice

PONMUND SATHAM

2 cups water

1 cup long-grain white rice

salt to taste

1 small onion

ghee

½ cup raisins

fresh cilantro

In this variation, a little sweetness of flavor and color is added by the use of onion and raisins.

1. Prepare the rice as stated in the recipe for simple rice, facing page.

2. Peel the onion and slice finely.

3. Melt 1 teaspoon of ghee in a heavy pan. Add the onion and fry gently until it is soft and golden brown.

4. Add the fried onion and the raisins to the rice 5 minutes before the end of cooking.

5. Serve garnished with fresh cilantro.

Rice with fresh lime

ELAMCHA SATHAM

2 cups water

1 cup long-grain white rice

salt to taste

1 small onion

ghee

1 teaspoon black mustard seeds

2 teaspoons lime juice, freshly squeezed

The lime juice adds a slightly fruity and tart flavor to the rice, and makes it a good accompaniment to rich dishes, or to fish.

1. Prepare the rice as stated in the recipe for simple rice, facing page.

2. While the rice is cooking, peel the onion and slice finely. Melt 1 teaspoon of ghee in a heavy pan. Add the onion and fry gently until it is soft and golden brown.

3. Add the black mustard seeds and continue cooking until they pop.

4. Add the freshly squeezed lime juice.

5. Add the fried onion mixture to the rice 5 minutes before the end of cooking, and stir gently.

Crunchy rice

UDUGAMALAM SATHAM

2 cups water

1 cup long-grain white rice

salt to taste

oil for deep frying

1 medium onion

½ cup unsalted roasted peanuts

Onions and peanuts add crunchiness to this rice. Buy roasted peanuts if you are in a hurry, or roast them yourself.

1. Peel and slice the onion into thin rings. Dry thoroughly with paper towel. Deep fry in hot oil until crisp. Remove and drain on paper towel. Set aside until needed.

2. Prepare the rice as stated in the recipe for simple rice (p. 14).

3. Garnish the drained cooked rice with the crisp fried onions and peanuts.

Tamarind rice

PULI SATHAM

2 cups water

1 cup long-grain white rice

salt to taste

1 tablespoon tamarind

2 dried red chilies

1 large onion

ghee or oil for frying

1 teaspoon black mustard seed

½–1 teaspoon fenugreek seed (to taste)

1 teaspoon tomato paste

The pods of the tamarind tree have a sweet yet tangy flavor and have preservative qualities as well (see Glossary). Here the sweet, fruity flavor of the tamarind is mingled with a touch of fire from the chilies, making an unforgettable combination of tastes. This rice is best when accompanying strong-flavored dishes, such as dark meat. Note: The fenugreek has a distinctive, bitter flavor – go cautiously unless you know you like it.

1. Prepare and cook the rice as described in the recipe for simple rice (p. 14).

2. Infuse the tamarind in ¼ cup of hot water. Strain after 5 minutes and set the liquid to one side.

3. Halve the dried red chilies and discard the seeds. Peel the onion and chop coarsely.

4. Fry the onion in 1 tablespoon of ghee or oil until soft and golden brown, then add the black mustard seeds. When they start to pop add the dried red chilies, the fenugreek seeds, the tamarind juice and the tomato paste. Bring to the boil and gently stir into the cooked, drained rice.

Saffron rice

KUNGAMAPU SATHAM

6 shallots

a pinch of saffron strands

1½ cups patna rice

6 tablespoons ghee

4 whole cloves

1 inch cinnamon stick

2 cardamom pods

⅔ cup cashew nuts

½ cup raisins

1 teaspoon salt (or to taste)

a pinch of turmeric

2 cups water

Garnish: 1 onion plus oil for deep frying

a sprig of fresh cilantro

Saffron rice has a royal touch. Yellow was the royal color of the Muslim kings, and Muslims who arrived in southern India from the northwest in the 14th century brought this dish with them. With its color and spice, and the sweetness and crunchiness of the cashew nuts, this is truly a dish fit for a king!

1. Peel and slice the shallots. Soak the saffron strands in a little water. Wash the rice and leave to one side.

2. Heat 2 tablespoons of ghee in a heavy-based saucepan and fry the rice until the ghee is absorbed. Remove and allow to cool a little.

3. Heat the remaining ghee in the same saucepan and fry the cloves, cinnamon bark, cardamom pods and cashew nuts until they begin to brown and to give off a lovely aroma. Add the sliced shallots and fry until soft. Then add the raisins, salt, turmeric and cold water and bring to a boil.

4. Lower the heat and mix in the rice. Cover the saucepan with a tight-fitting lid and cook until rice is soft and all water is absorbed (about 15 minutes).

5. ONION GARNISH: Peel and slice the onion into thin rings. Dry thoroughly with paper towel. Deep fry in hot oil until crisp. Remove and drain on paper towel. Set aside until needed.

6. Serve garnished with fresh cilantro and the crisp fried onions.

Yogurt rice

THAYAR SATHAM

2 cups water

1 cup long-grain white rice

salt to taste

1 fresh green chili or 1 dried red chili

½ inch fresh ginger

1 teaspoon black mustard seeds

ghee

asafetida (a piece the size of a raisin)

¼ plain yogurt

2 neem leaves (or bay leaves)

salt to taste

fresh cilantro

Yogurt is commonly used in Madras. Some houses and offices keep large red pots filled with lassi (a yogurt-based drink) which makes a cooling refresher when temperatures reach nearly 100°F. I serve dishes containing yogurt to anyone who is being introduced to spicy food for the first time. On such occasions, yogurt rice is an ideal choice. It is also a useful complement to more fiery or spicy dishes. It is usually served as a second course at large feasts, as it aids digestion.

1. Cook the rice as described in the recipe for simple rice (p. 14).

2. Deseed the chili and slice thinly. Peel and finely slice or grate the fresh ginger.

3. In a medium-sized pan, fry the black mustard seeds in 1 teaspoon of ghee until they pop. Next add the neem leaves and asafetida, and reduce the heat.

4. Add the sliced chili and the ginger, and continue to fry gently until an aroma arises. Gently stir in the yogurt and cook further for 1 minute.

5. Remove the yogurt mixture from the heat and pour over the cooked rice. Mix in with a fork.

6. The rice can be eaten hot or cold – with a fork, mix in the chopped cilantro before serving.

Tomato rice

TAKALI SATHAM

1 tablespoon tamarind

2 medium-sized ripe tomatoes

2 cups water

1 cup long-grain white rice

salt to taste

1 medium-sized onion

1 teaspoon ghee

1 tablespoon tomato paste

2 tablespoons butter

Red and yellow are symbolic colors in Tamil culture. The red-and-yellow flowers that cluster on the tamarind tree are echoed in the custom Tamil women observe of wearing red powder in their hair and a gold chain around their necks, both symbols of marriage. Combined sweetness and acidity enrich and enhance both a good marriage and a tempting dish. In this recipe, the rich red color and the sweetness of the tomatoes combine with the sweetness and acidity of the tamarind and onions to enrich the rice.

1. Infuse the tamarind in 2 tablespoons of hot water for 5 minutes. Strain the liquid and put to one side.

2. Scald the tomatoes with boiling water and remove the skins. Chop coarsely.

3. Peel and coarsely chop the onion.

4. Wash the rice thoroughly and cook as described in the recipe for simple rice (p. 14).

5. While the rice is cooking, fry the onion in the ghee over medium heat until it is soft and light brown. Add the tamarind liquid to the onion and let it boil gently for 5 minutes. Then add the tom-atoes and tomato paste. Lower the heat, cover the pan, and allow the sauce to simmer. It should become quite thick.

6. When the rice is very nearly cooked and most of its cooking water absorbed, add the tomato sauce and stir in gently. Serve.

Biryani

1 pound chicken pieces, lamb leg fillet, or jumbo shrimp (uncooked)

½ cup plain yogurt (not required for shrimp biryani)

1 large onion

3 green chilies

4 cloves garlic

1 inch fresh ginger

1 teaspoon chili powder

½ teaspoon turmeric

salt to taste

water

1½ cups basmati rice

ghee

8 cardamom pods

¼ inch cinnamon stick

4 whole cloves

2 cups fresh milk

FACING PAGE: *Biryani; yogurt relish,* tayar pachadi *(p. 115)*

Biryani is the most exotic rice dish in the whole of Indian cuisine, and basmati, the queen of rice, is used in its preparation. A rich dish of subtly spiced rice cooked together with shrimp, chicken, beef or lamb, biryani is generally served with only the simplest accompaniments: yogurt relish with tomato and cucumber, and mint chutney.

Biryani is served at large celebrations and religious festivals. On these occasions it is prepared by the men, out of doors in large clay pots over charcoal fires. At weddings, as members of the bridegroom's party arrive with trays of flowers – decorated with garlands and bearing the bride's wedding clothes – they will be greeted by the delicious scent of biryani wafting on the breeze, whetting their appetites and lingering in their minds during the ceremony.

In England, instead of the clay pot in the garden, I use a heavy casserole dish and cook the biryani in the oven. The result is just as good.

◆ Marinate overnight for best results.

1. Cut the meat into pieces about 1½ inches square and marinate in the yogurt, preferably overnight. (Skin can be left on the chicken or removed, as preferred.) Jumbo shrimp should be peeled, and deveined (make a slit in the back and remove the black thread), but should not be marinated.

2. Peel and quarter the onion, deseed the chilies. Finely chop or grind them together in a food processor. Leave to one side.

3. Peel the garlic and ginger; mince or grind finely using a food processor or mortar and pestle.

4. Place the marinated meat (reserving any remaining yogurt), or the prepared shrimp in a medium-sized, heavy saucepan with just enough water to cover. Add the chili powder, turmeric, ½ teaspoon salt (or to taste) and the water. Bring to the boil and simmer for 10 minutes (shrimp) to 20 minutes (meat). Reserve the stock.

5. Wash the rice and put to one side.

6. Melt 2 tablespoons of ghee in a large, heavy-based pan (preferably a cast-iron casserole) and fry the whole spices – cardamom pods, cinnamon stick and cloves – over medium heat. When a good aroma is released, add the ground onion and chilies, the garlic and ginger. Keep stirring, over medium heat, until their aroma starts to develop. Next add the washed rice. Lower the heat and continue to stir (if the mixture begins to stick, add a little more ghee).

7. Add the pieces of cooked meat or shrimp, 2 cups of milk (or mixture of milk and remaining yogurt) and 1 cup of the reserved stock. Cook for 5 minutes.

8. If necessary, transfer the mixture to a heavy casserole with a tight-fitting lid. Complete the cooking (covered) in a moderate oven (325°F) for 30 minutes (shrimp) or an hour (meat). Check at intervals – if at any stage there is insufficient liquid to cook the rice, add extra stock or water.

9. Serve warm, accompanied with yogurt relish (*tayar pachadi*, p. 115) and mint chutney (p. 116).

One story from Madras tells of a young heir who wanted to find the perfect wife. He decided that any woman who could produce a complete meal with two pounds of unthreshed rice would surely have all the qualities he desired, so disguising himself as an itinerant astrologer he set off in search of a bride.

During his travels he was shunned by many, but still he persevered, and one day he met a beautiful maiden whose parents had lost their wealth. Though he fell head over heels in love, he decided he should nonetheless put her to the rice cooking test he had planned, for he knew that an act without circumspection inevitably leads to regrets.

Ponni, the beautiful maiden, accepted his challenge and, the story goes, succeeded (though with a little help from her mother and servant). The servant washed and dried the rice, then Ponni, using the soles of her feet, separated the husks from the dried rice and sold them to the jewelers to use for polishing. With the money she received for the husks she sent her servant to buy firewood which she used to cook the rice. The ingenious young woman then sold the unburnt wood as charcoal, and bought vegetables, ghee, curds and tamarind in exchange.

As the day drew to a close the young man was served a feast of rice broth, vegetable pulao and spiced yogurt, with fragrant cool buttermilk to drink. He finished his dinner a most satisfied man, and the pair were duly married. Ever since then, this long-grain rice has been known as "Ponni."

Vegetable pulao

VEDANAYAGAM SHASTIKA

1 cup brown basmati rice

8 fresh green beans

4 small mushrooms

½ small cauliflower

1 carrot

2 medium onions

½ cup peas (fresh or frozen)

6 whole cloves

1 inch cinnamon bark

ghee

6 cardamom pods

1 teaspoon cumin seeds

1 teaspoon chili powder

2 cups water

salt to taste

sprig fresh cilantro

Tamilians celebrate numerous festivals throughout the year. At holi, celebrated in February, young unmarried girls and boys dress in white and throw colored powders at each other – green, red and cream. In this dish, often cooked at holi, the green of the peas and beans, the red of the carrots, the cream of the cauliflower and mushrooms reflect the colors thrown by the young people. It also has a touch of sharpness to remind us of their happiness and mischievousness. At holi, the cook traditionally offers the first mouthful of this dish to the one she loves best.

1. Wash the rice well, leave to drain.

2. Wash and slice the fresh green beans. Wash and cut the cauliflower into small florets. Wash or wipe and halve the mushrooms. Peel the carrot and onions and slice ⅛ inch thick. Shell the peas if necessary.

3. Grind the whole cloves and cinnamon stick very coarsely in a coffee grinder, or crush them with a mortar and pestle – this helps to release their flavors.

4. In a heavy-based saucepan or frying-pan with a tightly fitting lid, heat ¼ cup of ghee and fry the cardamom pods, the crushed whole cloves and cinnamon stick until an aroma arises.

5. Then add the sliced onions and the cumin seeds, and cook until the onions are soft and golden. Mix in the chili powder.

6. Stir in the prepared vegetables and cook for 2–5 minutes over low heat.

7. Mix in the washed rice and fry, stirring, until all the ghee has been absorbed. Add the water and salt to taste.

8. Cover the pan with a tight-fitting lid. Raise the heat and bring the ingredients to the boil.

9. Lower the heat as far as possible and simmer, covered, until the rice and vegetables are soft. It will take approximately 20 minutes.

Alternatively, the pulao may be transferred to a moderately hot oven (325°F) and cooked for around 20 minutes.

10. Garnish with cilantro before serving. The pulao is good accompanied by coconut chutney or mint chutney (p. 116).

Shrimp pulao

ARUMAINAYAGAM CHITTARANAM

Large and exceptionally tasty shrimp are caught in the waters around Madras. The combination of delicious juicy shrimp and the fragrance of the spices makes this a remarkable pulao dish. It's best to use fresh shrimp if you can, preferably uncooked (grayish in color, rather than pink). Frozen shrimp are often salted, so to reduce the saltiness let them thaw then rinse well before cooking.

1 pound large shrimp, preferably uncooked

salt

½ teaspoon turmeric

1 teaspoon chili powder

2 medium onions

1 cup rice

1 inch cinnamon stick

4 whole cloves

1 teaspoon cumin seeds

4 cardamom pods

2 cups water

sprig fresh cilantro

1. Shell and wash the shrimp. Marinate them with 1 teaspoon of salt (exclude salt if using frozen shrimp that are salted), turmeric and chili powder for 20 minutes.

2. Peel the onions and chop coarsely.

3. Wash the rice and leave to one side. Grind the cinnamon stick and cloves in a coffee grinder or with a mortar and pestle.

4. In a large frying pan or large iron casserole (choose one with a tightly fitting lid) fry the marinated shrimp in 2 tablespoons of ghee until nearly done (around 5 minutes for raw shrimp, 3 minutes for cooked ones, depending on size) then remove from the ghee and leave to one side.

5. In the same ghee fry the coarsely chopped onions until they are soft. Add the cumin seeds, cardamom pods, ground cloves and cinnamon stick, and fry until there is an aroma.

6. Add the washed rice and fry until all the ghee has been absorbed, and the rice is translucent. Add the cold water, a teaspoon of salt and the fried shrimp. Cover the pan, raise the heat slightly and bring to the boil.

7. Lower the heat as low as possible and simmer, tightly covered, for 20 minutes. The rice should be cooked and soft (if it becomes dry before it is cooked, add a small amount of cold water and continue cooking). Alternatively, the pulao may be transferred to a moderately hot oven (375°F) and cooked for around 20 minutes.

8. Serve garnished with chopped cilantro.

Drying the harvest

BREADS AND PANCAKES

Long before Western-style loaves came to Madras in the 19th century, the usual forms of bread were *chappatis, parathas, rotis* and *pooris* – all flat, unleavened breads, generally made with *atta* flour (finely ground whole wheat flour). In Madras, the flour is often freshly ground at home, using a large grinding stone.

These Indian breads are all eaten while warm and freshly cooked, and are generally used to scoop up foods they are eaten with. Although these breads go with many different dishes, they are usually eaten with their traditional accompaniments: chappatis with *dhall*; paratha with shrimp; poori with potatoes.

Chappatis, parathas and rotis are all baked on a griddle (or in a heavy frying pan). Chappatis are the simplest bread, and quick to make: they are about 6 inches in diameter, thin and soft. Parathas are a layered bread, rich in ghee and rather filling, while Madras rotis (which are different from rotis in the north) are made with white flour and are richer still. They are sometimes cooked with a delicious creamy filling of ground meat and nuts to become a meal in themselves.

Chappatis, parathas and rotis are eaten mainly in the evening instead of rice, though in some Tamil homes both bread and rice are served in the evening and it is a matter of preference what one has.

Note: These breads start to dry rapidly if they are not eaten straight from the pan, but keep well if they are wrapped in foil immediately (you can put them in the oven to keep warm, or set them back on the griddle, which will retain some of its heat after cooking).

Pooris are prepared rather like chappatis, but then deep fried so they puff up into a light, soft bread. Sometimes pooris are eaten for breakfast as a change from more usual *dosais* (which are like pancakes), *appams* or *idlis*.

Dosais, appams and idlis are all made from batters of rice and grams (legumes) or coconut, allowed to stand overnight so they begin to ferment – this gives them a distinctive and delicious (almost yogurt-like) tang. The idli batter is steamed to make little rice cakes; the dosais, however, are magnificent pale-golden pancakes (street vendors make them 18 inches across), very thin, crispy on the surface yet slightly spongy inside. Appams (also called hoppers) are pancakes with a soft middle but a crisp, lacy-textured surface – they are a great favorite with Tamilians.

Simple flat bread

CHAPPATIS

MAKES 8

2 cups atta flour (see Glossary)

½ cup lukewarm water

¼ cup ghee, butter or margarine, melted

½–1 teaspoon salt (to taste)

oil

This is the simplest of all breads, made just of atta (a fine whole wheat) flour, ghee, and water. Making chappatis is an extremely quick and simple process, since the dough does not require fermentation, although you do need to prepare it at least half an hour in advance. The chappatis are rolled before cooking (traditionally, the art of rolling chappatis was said to help young women maintain their figures but chappati presses were brought on the market to save time).

In Madras, the high air temperatures mean that water is usually naturally warm – when I moved to England I learned I had to warm the water first in order to get the dough to work properly (it should be lukewarm: when tested with your finger it should feel neither hot nor cold). It is also important to heat the ghee until it melts but does not become hot – otherwise it will start to cook the flour when you add it. If atta flour (also sold as chappati flour) is unavailable, try using whole wheat pastry flour [available in health food stores].

The instructions are for making chappati dough by hand, although a food processor can also be used.

1. Measure the flour and salt into a bowl. Make a well in the flour and add the melted ghee. Gradually add the water, mixing with the fingers until a soft dough is formed. (The quantity of water required depends on the flour – use slightly less or more to get the right, soft, consistency.)

2. Knead for 10 minutes (3 minutes in a food processor), then form into a ball. Wrap in a damp cloth and allow to stand for at least half an hour before using.

3. On a floured board form the dough into eight walnut-sized balls and roll them into rounds 5 inches in diameter (keep covered with the dampened cloth to stop them from drying out).

4. Grease a griddle or heavy frying pan (preferably cast iron) with a drop of oil, and heat. With the cloth, dampen both sides of the first chappati, then place it on the griddle. Press it down with a spatula, and keep it on the move so that it does not stick. When the first side is pale brown (with a few brown spots) turn and cook on the other side. Remove from the griddle.

5. Repeat the process until all the chappatis are made. They should be served immediately after cooking, or immediately wrapped in foil and kept warm, otherwise they will begin to harden.

FACING PAGE: *Dosais (p. 34) with drumstick sambar (p. 122) and coconut chutney (p. 116)*

Puffed bread

POORIS

MAKES 12–15

½ cup all-purpose flour

2 cups atta flour (see Glossary)

1 teaspoon salt

1 teaspoon baking soda

¼ cup ghee, butter or margarine, melted

6–8 tablespoons water

oil for frying

In September each year Tamilians celebrate the Hindu festival Navaratri (which literally means "good night," when prayers are said for children. On this special day of the year, children are allowed to stay up all night, playing until morning with special little dolls that are dressed in fine clothes, and enjoying treats and special snacks. In the evening young girls help their mothers make the dough for pooris.

This bread is deep-fried in a kadai, *or wok, to form little light, wheaten puffballs. A deep fryer may also be used. The pooris puff and bubble up when they are placed in the hot oil, and should be turned over and removed with a metal strainer immediately or they will become too crispy. The oil in the wok should not be allowed to get smoking hot or the pooris will burn.*

The dough should be prepared at least an hour before use, and pooris should be eaten straight away as they collapse when cold.

1. Sift both the flours into a mixing bowl. Add the salt and baking soda. Make a well in the flour and add the melted ghee. Gradually add the water. Mix the flour with fingers to make a soft dough. (A food processor can also be used.)

2. Knead the dough for 10 minutes (3 minutes in a food processor), then form it into a ball. Wrap in a damp cloth and allow to stand for at least an hour before using.

3. Form the dough into 12–15 evenly sized balls. On a floured board flatten and roll each ball of dough into a 2-inch disk, then place on a tray. (Keep them covered so they do not dry out.)

4. Heat a few inches of oil in a wok or deep fryer (the temperature can be tested by dropping a small cube of bread into the oil – it should rise to the top). Drop in one poori at a time and press down into the oil with a wooden spoon. Turn it over and as soon as it puffs up remove and drain on paper towel. Serve at once or wrap in foil to keep warm.

Layered wheat bread

PARATHAS

MAKES 12

3 cups atta flour (see Glossary)

¼ teaspoon salt

¾ cup ghee, melted

1 cup boiling water

Parathas are flat, layered wheat bread, one of the most popular alternatives to rice as an accompaniment to Tamilian dishes of all kinds. They are also sold as snacks: at Hindu festivals vendors do a roaring trade selling parathas to the hungry visitors.

Parathas are small (about 3 inches across) but heavier than chappatis and quite filling. They are best dipped in the accompanying dish, though some people prefer to roll them up with a little of the food wrapped in them. However you eat them, I hope you enjoy them as much as I do.

◆ The dough needs to be started about an hour before it is cooked.

1. Sift the flour and salt into a mixing bowl (a food processor can also be used) and make a well in the center. Pour 1 tablespoon of ghee into the well in the flour, and mix well. Pour in a quarter of the boiling water to form a soft dough that shouldn't be too sticky. Knead the dough well for 15 minutes (5 minutes in a food processor), and form it into a ball. Sprinkle with 1 tablespoon of water, cover with a damp cloth and leave for 30 minutes.

2. On a floured surface, roll out the dough into a long sausage. Divide the dough into 12 portions. Roll each one into a thin disk 5 inches in diameter.

3. Remelt the remaining ghee if necessary. Brush the surface of each disk with melted ghee and fold it in half, brush with ghee again and fold to a quarter. Form each quarter into a ball again. Slightly flatten each ball with the palm of your hand, and roll out again to a disk 3 inches in diameter.

4. Heat a heavy-based cast-iron frying pan or a griddle, greased with ghee. Cook each paratha on one side, then turn it over (spreading more ghee on the griddle before replacing the paratha). Cook until both sides are crisp and golden brown. Serve at once or keep warm wrapped in foil.

Rich white bread

VASANTHA'S ROTI

MAKES 12

2 cups all-purpose white flour

¼ teaspoon salt

1½ cups ghee

¼ cup boiling water

Roti is a nutritious and filling layered bread made of all-purpose white flour. Originally it came from Ootacamund, up in the Nilgiri Hills in western Tamil Nadu, home of the Todar people who eat it to keep out the cold in winter. Roti is traditionally cooked on a heavy griddle over a charcoal fire, and street vendors practice their showmanship by tossing the dough around as they work it. However, a rolling-pin and a griddle or heavy-based frying pan will also produce excellent results. This recipe was taught me by my aunt Vasantha.

◆ The dough needs to be prepared 2 or 3 hours before cooking.

1. Sift the flour and salt into a mixing bowl. A food processor can also be used. Make a well in the flour and pour in a third of the melted ghee. Mix well and gradually add water until a soft dough is formed. Knead for 15 minutes (5 minutes in a food processor) until the dough is of silky consistency. Form into a ball, cover with a damp cloth, and set aside for 2–3 hours for the dough to soften.

2. Divide the dough into 12 equal-sized balls. On a well-floured board roll each ball into a disk 10 inches in diameter. Sprinkle with a teaspoon of melted ghee and fold the edges into the middle to form a square. Sprinkle with a little flour and roll out slightly to 5 inches diameter. Keep covered so the dough does not dry out.

3. Heat a griddle or heavy-based frying pan (preferably cast iron), and grease with a little ghee. Place a piece of dough on the griddle and cook until it is slightly brown on one side. Turn it over and brown slightly.

4. Remove the roti and spread a teaspoonful of ghee on the griddle. Replace the roti and cook on one side for 2 minutes. Remove the roti, spread another teaspoonful of ghee and cook the second side for 2 minutes. Remove and keep warm, wrapped in foil.

5. Repeat the process until all the dough is used.

MAKES 12

Dough made as in the recipe for roti, facing page (this needs to stand for 2–3 hours before use)

1 large onion

2 green chilies

¼ inch fresh ginger

2 cloves garlic

1 cup fresh spinach leaves

¼ teaspoon turmeric

1 teaspoon chili powder

2 teaspoons ground cumin

ghee

¼ inch cinnamon stick

¼ pound lean ground lamb

2 tablespoons cashew nuts

½ teaspoon salt

¼-inch cube coconut cream or 2 teaspoons coconut milk powder

1 cup ghee for cooking

MAIDA'S STUFFED ROTI

This is a delicious elaboration on the recipe opposite. The filling is fresh, lean ground lamb mixed with spinach and cashew nuts, all cooked together in a creamy, spicy sauce.

Stuffed rotis are considered to be a meal on their own – the only accompaniment would be a vegetable dish. Actual cooking time is very quick, about 5 minutes for each roti.

THE STUFFING

1. Peel and chop the onion coarsely. Deseed and chop the green chilies. Peel the ginger and garlic and chop very finely. Wash the spinach and chop coarsely.

2. Make a paste with the turmeric, chili powder, ground cumin and 1 tablespoon of water.

3. Heat 1 teaspoon of ghee in a saucepan. When the ghee is melted add the cinnamon stick. When there is a slight aroma add the chopped onion, and continue to fry until it has softened but not browned. Then add the ginger, garlic and chilies. Keep frying for another minute before adding the prepared spice paste and salt; keep stirring until the aroma is released.

4. Add the ground lamb and 1 tablespoon of water. Cover, and cook over medium heat for 10 minutes. Meanwhile, fry the cashew nuts in 1 teaspoon of ghee until golden, and set aside.

5. Lower the heat under the lamb mixture, and add the coconut (cream or milk powder) and spinach. Continue to cook, uncovered, for about 5 minutes or until most of the moisture has gone. Stir in the fried cashews. Remove the pan from the heat and leave to cool.

ASSEMBLY AND COOKING

1. Divide the dough into 12 equal-sized balls. On a well-floured board roll each ball into a disk 10 inches in diameter. Spread with a teaspoon of melted ghee (right to the edges), then spread the middle 4 inches with 2 teaspoons of the filling. Fold the edges of the dough into the middle to cover the ingredients and make a square

One of the most famous seasonal festivals in southern India occurs in July at Kanchipuram, famous for its silk saris. This is very much a women's festival when the women wear green saris to welcome the monsoon rains. Here numerous vendors sell their stuffed roti to the crowds of visitors who come to see the Goddess Parvati, goddess of the monsoon, carried in procession accompanied by elephants bearing ceremonial umbrellas.

about 4 inches across. Sprinkle the upper surface with a little flour and press slightly.

2. Heat a griddle or heavy-based frying pan (preferably cast iron), and grease with a little ghee. Place the filled dough in the frying pan (folds upwards) and fry until lightly browned. Turn it over and brown slightly on the other side.

3. Remove the roti and spread a teaspoon of ghee on the griddle. Replace the roti and cook on one side for 2 minutes. Remove the roti, spread the griddle with more ghee and cook the other side of the roti for 2 minutes. Remove and serve or keep warm in the oven, covered with foil.

4. Repeat the process until all the dough and filling are used.

Rice and gram pancakes

DOSAIS

Dosais are beautiful, pale-golden pancakes, crispy on the surface yet slightly spongy inside. The best ones are made with a lot of ghee to ensure they are thin and crisp – ones made by the Madras dosai vendors are enormous, up to 18 inches across, but homemade ones are about 8 inches in diameter. Dosais can be eaten as an accompaniment, to scoop up other foods, but are most often eaten for breakfast, together with sambar (p. 122), and coconut chutney (p. 116) – see photograph on p. 29.

Dosais can be made with a variety of batters, each giving a slightly different texture or color, but the traditional mix is of the rice and split grams used in this recipe. The mixture of rice and split black grams is prepared in advance and allowed to ferment overnight, and is ground to a batter the next day (traditionally, young girls were said to have improved their figures and their posture by the heavy job of grinding the rice with a heavy granite pestle in a mortar – a

MAKES ABOUT 12 8-INCH
DOSAIS

¾ cup cleaned split black grams
(urad dhall)

1¼ cups long-grain white rice

¼ cup water

ghee

1 teaspoon baking soda

1–1½ teaspoons salt

oil

*method still used by Tamil women in villages). The food processor is a
great help.*

*In Madras, dosais are cooked on a dosai kalu, which translated
means "dosai stone." The dosai kalu is in fact made of cast iron and
needs to be kept clean and oiled at all times. A good substitute is a
heavy griddle or cast-iron frying pan, both of which distribute the
heat well. The pan is wiped with a cloth dipped in oil before the mix-
ture is ladled into it.*

*Making good dosais is an art, and like any pancake making needs
a little practice. They are well worth it.*

◆ This recipe requires 2 standing periods (6 hours for the grain mix-
ture, and at least 12 hours for the finished batter).

1. Soak the black grams (urad dhall) and long-grain rice separately
for at least 6 hours, preferably overnight. Strain.

2. Grind the soaked rice in a food processor, adding a little water at
a time, until the mixture becomes a smooth batter.

3. Grind the grams in the same way, then mix the rice batter with
the split gram batter. Beat in the baking soda and salt for 5 min-
utes. Leave in a warm place, loosely covered, for 12 hours for it to
ferment.

4. Heat a heavy-based frying pan (preferably with an 8-inch base).
Place a little oil in a bowl. Grease the frying pan with a cloth dipped
in the oil.

5. Before using the batter, stir once with a spoon. Ladle 2–3 table-
spoons of batter into the center of the frying pan and distribute it
evenly with the rounded base of the ladle, working it outward using
circular movements until a pancake 8 inches in diameter is formed.
Trickle a little melted ghee round the edges of the dosai, to help
make it crisp. Cook for 2 minutes until it is brown. Then turn it over
and cook for another 2 minutes. Add another drop of ghee round
the edges again. The dosai is ready to be eaten. Serve right away.

6. Before making the next dosai, wipe the frying pan again with the
oil-soaked cloth.

Stuffed crisp pancakes

MASALA DOSAIS

MAKES ABOUT 12 8-INCH
MASALA DOSAIS

FOR THE DOSAI BATTER

½ cup cleaned split black grams
(urad dhall) (see Glossary)

1½ cups long-grain white rice

1 teaspoon fenugreek seeds

¼ cup water

ghee

1 teaspoon baking soda

1–1½ teaspoons salt

FOR THE FILLING

3 small potatoes

2 small carrots

2–3 fresh green beans

3 shallots or 1 small onion

1 green chili

ghee

1 teaspoon black mustard seeds

1 tablespoon split cleaned black
grams (urad dhall)

¼ teaspoon turmeric

*Masala dosais are made as in the previous recipe (with slightly differ-
ent proportions of rice and grams), but are rolled up, and have a
vegetable masala filling (recipe below). Alternatively, the dosais can
be filled with masala potato (p. 56). They are served with sambar
(p. 122) and coconut chutney (p. 116).*

*This is a dish that is particularly associated with marriage. For
instance, it is traditional for the families of the bride and groom to
choose the couple's wedding clothes. Choosing a wedding sari is fun
but backbreaking, since the women have to sit on carpets while the
gold and silver saris are spread out on long, low platforms to be scru-
tinized. Afterwards, everyone appreciates going to a restaurant to
have a restorative masala dosai!*

◆ This recipe requires 2 standing periods (6 hours for the grain
mixture, and at least 12 hours for the finished batter).

THE BATTER

1. Place the split cleaned black grams (urad dhall) in a bowl and
cover with water. Place the long-grain rice and fenugreek seeds in a
separate bowl and cover with water. Allow the grams and rice to
soak for at least 6 hours, preferably overnight.

2. Strain the soaked rice, then blend in a food processor, adding the
water a little at a time, until the mixture becomes a smooth batter.
Grind the grams in the same way.

3. Mix the rice batter with the split gram batter. Add the baking soda
and salt and beat for 5 minutes. Cover loosely and leave in a warm
place overnight for the batter to ferment.

4. The next day the dosai batter is ready for use.

THE FILLING

1. Peel the potatoes and carrots, and dice finely. Parboil them for
1–2 minutes, drain and set aside. Wash and cut the fresh green

beans into ¼-inch lengths. Peel and slice the shallots into fine slices. Deseed and finely chop the chili.

2. Heat 1 teaspoon of ghee in a saucepan and fry the black mustard seeds until they pop. Then add the grams and cook until they turn brown.

3. Then add the sliced shallot, chopped green chili and turmeric. When an aroma rises add the potatoes, carrots and beans. Add ¼ cup of water, cover the pan and cook over low heat until the vegetables are soft. Remove the saucepan and leave to cool.

THE DOSAIS AND ASSEMBLY

1. Heat a heavy-based frying pan, preferably 8 inches in diameter. Place a little oil in a bowl. Grease the frying pan with a cloth dipped in the oil.

2. Stir the batter gently before use. Ladle 2–3 tablespoons of batter into the center of the frying pan and distribute it evenly with the rounded base of the ladle, working it outward using circular movements until a pancake 8 inches in diameter is formed. Trickle a little melted ghee round the edges of the dosai to make it crisp. Cook for 2 minutes until it is brown. Then turn it over and cook until slightly brown.

3. Place a tablespoon of filling in the center of the dosai. Cook for another minute. Then roll the dosai to form a cylinder. Remove the dosai from the pan with a flat metal spatula and serve at once.

4. Before making the next dosai, wipe the frying pan again with the oil-soaked cloth.

Rice pancakes

APPAMS

MAKES ABOUT 15

1 cup long-grain white rice

⅓ cup grated coconut or
1 tablespoon coconut milk
powder

1 teaspoon baking soda

salt to taste

oil for the pan

Tamilians are not only divided into castes, but into different communities, and marriages between these different groups are not encouraged. One community is well known as tree climbers: they climb the palmyra palms to tap the toddy. *This liquid is sweet and nonalcoholic when it is drunk fresh (left overnight it ferments and becomes alcoholic).*

Appams – pancakes with a lovely, lacy pattern on the outside, and spongy inside – were introduced by this community and traditionally fresh toddy is added to help the batter to ferment. The outer edges are dry and crisp when hot, but flop when cold. Thus the local nickname of "floppers." They go well with thick coconut milk (see Glossary) sweetened with sugar. Appams are normally made in a small wok – a crêpe pan can also be used, though it won't give the distinctive concave shape.

◆ The rice needs to stand for 3 hours and the batter overnight.

1. Wash the rice and soak it for at least 3 hours. Grind with water in an electric blender.

2. Mix the grated coconut or coconut milk powder with ¼ cup of hot water to make coconut milk (if using fresh coconut, strain the liquid after 5 minutes, and discard the pulp).

3. Add the coconut milk, baking soda and salt to the batter. Mix in well and leave overnight.

4. Whisk the batter well before making the appams – it should have a smooth, pancake-batter consistency .

5. Grease the wok with a cloth dipped in oil. Place a tablespoonful of batter in the heated wok. Tilt the wok slightly all round so that the batter clings to the sides, making a 5-inch appam (some batter will pool in the middle). Cook until the sides are crisp – the middle will be soft. Serve hot immediately (or keep covered on a warmed plate for a few minutes).

Steamed dumplings

TIDLI IDLIS

MAKES ABOUT 24
DUMPLINGS (SERVES 6–8)

1 cup cleaned split black grams
(urad dhall)

1¼ cups long-grain white rice

ghee

1 teaspoon baking soda

1 teaspoon salt

Idlis are light, fluffy steamed rice-and-gram dumplings. Accompanied by coffee, they are mainly eaten for breakfast, though restaurants in Madras serve them as a snack throughout the day. They are sometimes served with coconut chutney (p. 116) or sambar (p. 122), or with sugar.

Though the batter needs to stand overnight, the cooking itself is simple and takes less than 15 minutes.

Idlis are cooked in utensils similar to egg poachers. In fact an egg poacher will do the job very well, or you can buy an idli steamer from a specialty store.

◆ The mixture has to ferment overnight.

1. Wash both the cleaned split black grams and the rice, and put them to soak, separately, in water overnight or for 6 hours.

2. Strain the rice, and grind it in a food processor with 2 tablespoons of water, making a coarse batter. Remove and set aside.

3. Strain the grams and grind in a food processor with a little water – this should make a smooth batter. Mix the two batters together and stir in the salt and baking soda. Leave to stand overnight, loosely covered, in a warm place to ferment.

4. Grease the egg poacher or idli tray with ghee. Place 1 tablespoon of idli batter in the middle of each compartment, and smooth it with the back of the spoon. Cover, and steam the idlis for 10–15 minutes. They will rise and can be tested with a toothpick (if it comes out clean the idlis are cooked). Serve immediately.

Dawn is regarded as an auspicious time for house-moving. The night before, a religious token and a jar of salt are left in the new house, for luck. Next morning the new householder goes to the temple and brings back a young calf (symbolizing the goddess Indra). He leads it through the house to the sound of musical pipes. The wife boils milk (also a symbol of the goddess) for coffee, for her breakfast guests. As idlis contain auspicious black grams, they are a dish served at a special breakfast like this.

VEGETABLES

Tamil Nadu is officially a Hindu state, and as the Hindu Brahmin caste is vegetarian, vegetables and legumes are the basis of the Tamil diet. Many people do eat meat and fish but even so, these are not the centerpiece of a meal the way they traditionally are in the West. For everybody, Hindu or not, at least one meal a day will be vegetarian, hence the abundance of vegetable dishes in Tamil cuisine.

Custom, too, plays an important role in the Tamilians' diet: many Tamilians have a vegetable meal on the eve of an important occasion, as abstention from meat is associated with purity.

A vegetarian meal generally consists of five or six vegetables with rice and dhall (a lentil dish, p. 62), chutney or relish, and yogurt. Two hard vegetables, such as carrots, potatoes or pumpkin, will be combined with two fresh leafy ones, such as spinach or cabbage, and perhaps also with juicy eggplant, plump squash or beans. So strong is the division of vegetables into the "hard" and "leafy" groups that each type has its own name, and there is no one Tamilian word for "vegetables."

Thanks to the climate and good soil, an excellent variety of vegetables is available cheaply throughout the year. Some are sold from carts wheeled along the streets, others at the vegetable markets, still more by women who carry on their heads baskets of home-grown produce.

Vegetables are generally cooked quickly, using a traditional method of braising and steaming, so that they retain their full flavor and a little crispness.

Charred sweet peppers

CHUTTA PERISA MALIGAI

6 sweet peppers (as wide a range of colors as possible)

2 medium onions

1 clove of garlic

2 tomatoes

ghee

1 teaspoon black mustard seeds

1 teaspoon lovage seeds

2 cardamom pods

½ teaspoon chili powder

¼ teaspoon turmeric

¼ teaspoon salt (or to taste)

2 tablespoons brown sugar (optional)

Tamils still use the ancient method of cooking this dish in the charcoal ashes of a clay oven, and this certainly imparts a flavor that is difficult to achieve with modern methods, although you can get a similar effect by searing the vegetables under a broiler. The result is that the differing flavors of the peppers are retained, with a touch of the barbecue added. Removing the charred skins is a fiddly job and takes some time. The vegetables are then chopped and sautéed. (If available, use a mixture of peppers, including white, orange and purple.)

Sugar is often added, enhancing the natural sweetness of the peppers and making this a good complement to more fiery dishes. (For a crunchier texture, a few roasted sunflower seeds or unsalted cashew nuts may be added before serving.)

1. Char the skins of the peppers: either on a hot charcoal barbecue, under a hot broiler (quarter them first and lay them skin uppermost) or by holding them in a gas flame using two forks. The skin will scorch and blister. Once cool enough to touch, remove the skin and any remaining stalk or seeds. Cut the pulp into ½-inch squares.

2. Peel the onions and chop coarsely. Peel and crush the garlic. Wash and roughly chop the tomatoes. Put aside.

3. In a saucepan heat 2 teaspoons of ghee and fry the black mustard seeds, lovage seeds and the cardamom pods. When the black mustard seeds pop add the sliced onions and crushed garlic, and fry until soft and golden brown. Add the chili powder and turmeric and fry for 2 minutes. Then add the chopped tomatoes, salt and sugar. Finally add the peppers and fry, stirring, for 5 minutes. Cover and cook for a further 3–5 minutes to allow the flavors to blend.

Fried small purple eggplant

KATRIKA PORIYAL

1 medium onion

1 green chili

2 small eggplants (about 8 ounces)

1 tablespoon cilantro

ghee

1 teaspoon chili powder

½ teaspoon turmeric

salt to taste

There are many varieties of eggplant, or brinjal (the Tamil name is katrika) in Madras: long green ones, big purple ones and small round lilac ones. The long white eggplants are usually added to sambar (see p. 122). For this recipe the small round purple eggplants are best, being sweeter than the other varieties, but any sort can be used.

1. Peel and chop the onion coarsely. Deseed and slice the green chili. Wash and dice the eggplant. Coarsely chop the cilantro.

2. Fry the onion in 1 teaspoon of ghee until soft.

3. Continue frying and add the chili powder and the turmeric. They should quickly brown and cook. Then add the cubed eggplant, salt, cilantro and green chili. Stir for about 5 minutes.

4. Add ¼ cup of water, cover the pan, and cook until the eggplant and onions are soft and moist (10–15 minutes). Serve garnished with cilantro.

Snow peas with ginger and chili

PADAIPAI AVARAKA

¾ cup snow peas

1 inch fresh ginger

1 green chili

oil

1 teaspoon chili powder

½ teaspoon salt (or to taste)

The job of trimming the snow peas is often Grandma's task. Snow peas are commonly served as an accompanying vegetable, or cooked together with fried beef or lamb. In this recipe, the ginger and chili combine beautifully with the snow peas.

1. Trim the washed snow peas. Peel and slice the ginger. Deseed the chili and slice finely.

2. In 1 teaspoon of oil fry the chili powder for a few seconds. Then add the whole snow peas and stir them in.

3. Add the sliced fresh ginger and green chili. Add 2 tablespoons water and salt. Cover, and cook until the snow peas are tender (5–10 minutes).

Though only Brahmins are usually strictly vegetarian, vegetarian traditions are significant for everybody. On religious days, for example, only legumes, vegetables and rice are eaten (some Christians practice this on Good Friday). And during pregnancy or after the birth of a child, vegetables and legumes are considered very important sources of nutrients. After the death of a member of the family, no meat is eaten for 14 days.

Green peas with lovage seeds

NAGAPATINAM PATANI

1 small onion

1 clove garlic

¼ inch fresh ginger

1 green chili

½ pound shelled fresh garden peas

ghee

1 teaspoon lovage seeds

½ teaspoon ground coriander

salt to taste

cilantro

Tamilians traded with ancient Greece and Rome; among the foods enterprising traders brought East were peas, and Tamilian women cooked them in their own way, with a touch of spice. Tamilians can buy shelled garden peas in vegetable markets today, and in Ootacamund large baskets of peas can be seen in summer. The lovage seeds add a hint of licorice to this extremely simple dish. Tender fresh fava beans can be substituted.

1. Peel and slice the onion. Peel and chop the garlic and ginger. De-seed and slice the fresh green chili.

2. Shell the peas. Heat 1 teaspoon of ghee and fry the lovage seeds over medium heat. Add the onion and fry until slightly golden, then add the ginger and garlic.

3. Next add the peas, then the ground coriander, salt to taste and 1½ tablespoons of water. Turn down to very low heat, cover the pan and cook until the peas are soft (about 10 minutes). Just at the end of cooking add the coarsely chopped cilantro.

FACING PAGE: *Duck with coconut (p. 95), cabbage with onions and black mustard seeds (p. 53), green peas with lovage seeds and chappatis (p. 27)*

Just okra

TANKASI VENDAKAI

½ pound okra

1 medium onion

1 teaspoon oil

1 teaspoon black mustard seeds

2 tablespoons milk

salt to taste

The Tamil name for this vegetable is vendakai, *though we often call it ladies' fingers. Here the okra are sliced and cooked in a mild, creamy sauce – the black mustard seeds release the flavor of the vegetable. This is extremely quick and simple to prepare, the most time-consuming part being the trimming.*

1. Wash and trim the okra. Split them in half lengthwise (optional) and cut them into ¼-inch lengths.

2. Peel the onion and chop it coarsely.

3. In a little oil over medium heat fry the onion until soft.

4. Add the black mustard seeds and fry until they pop. Add the okra.

5. Fry the okra with the onion for a minute, salt to taste. Then gradually add the milk. Lower the heat.

6. Cover tightly and cook for 5–10 minutes until the okra is cooked but still slightly firm. If the okra becomes dry during cooking, add a little water.

Spiced okra

TIRUNVELI VENDAKAI

Sometimes Tamilians prefer vegetables to be a little spicier, especially when part of a vegetarian dinner. The rich tamarind sauce used here produces a dish very different from "just okra."

½ pound okra

1 medium red onion

1 clove garlic

2 red chilies

1 tablespoon tamarind

oil or ghee

salt to taste

¼ teaspoon sugar

1. Trim the washed okra and cut into ¼-inch slices.

2. Peel and quarter the onion, peel the garlic. Deseed the red chilies. Blend together roughly in a food processor (or chop finely and grind in a mortar and pestle).

3. Infuse the tamarind in 3 tablespoons of hot water for 5 minutes. Mix well and strain. Set the liquid to one side.

4. Heat 1 tablespoon of oil or ghee, and fry the ground ingredients over medium heat until fragrant. Then add the okra and fry for 1–2 minutes. Add the tamarind juice, salt and sugar. Lower the heat, cover and simmer for 5–10 minutes. Remove and serve hot.

Fried long beans

VEDDATHANAI PORICHAR BEANS

1 pound long beans

1 medium red onion

oil for frying

1 teaspoon chili powder

¼ teaspoon turmeric

½ teaspoon salt (or to taste)

Long beans resemble French or green beans, but are three or four times the length, and are a favorite in India and Southeast Asia. They are tender when light green, and firm, but are past their best when they start to turn yellow. If long beans are unavailable, French or green beans can be substituted. Here the traditional method of braising and steaming the vegetables is used.

1. Wash the long beans and cut them into 1-inch lengths. Peel the onion and chop coarsely.

2. Fry the onion in 2 teaspoons of oil until soft. Then add the long beans. Add the salt, turmeric and chili powder. Cover the pan and cook over a low heat for 10 minutes, gradually adding ¼ cup of water. The beans should be tender but not overly soft.

Jiji's beans

1 small red onion

½ pound green beans

ghee

½ teaspoon cumin seeds

½ cup milk

2 tablespoons plain yogurt

½ teaspoon chili powder

¼ teaspoon turmeric

pinch salt

1 teaspoon ground coriander

This dish is from Pondicherry, near Madras, where the French East India Company was based, and was taught to me by my sister. Whereas most Tamilians use coconut milk for sauces, Tamilians in this region prefer fresh milk and yogurt in their sauces – influenced perhaps by the cream-based sauces so loved by the French. This recipe uses dwarf, French or green beans, which are mainly grown around Pondicherry – perhaps another legacy of the French.

1. Peel the onion. Cut in half and slice finely into half-rings. Slice the beans in half lengthwise.

2. Heat 2 teaspoons of ghee in a large, heavy pan over medium heat. Add the cumin seeds and fry lightly. Add the milk, then gradually mix in the yogurt and whisk gently.

3. Add the chili powder, turmeric and salt. Simmer for 5 minutes.

4. Add the ground coriander, the beans and the onions. Cover and simmer for 5 minutes, then add 2 tablespoons of hot water. Cover again and cook for a further 5–10 minutes until the beans and onions are just soft (or to taste).

Working the land

Drumsticks

MAMMALAM MURUNGAKAI

1 tablespoon tamarind

4 tender drumsticks

1 medium onion

¼ inch fresh ginger

1 clove garlic

ghee or oil

1 teaspoon mustard seeds

½ teaspoon turmeric

2 tomatoes

1 teaspoon light brown sugar

¼ teaspoon salt (or to taste)

When I moved to England and asked for drumsticks at a vegetable store I was amazed to be sent to the butcher's for them! Drumsticks as I knew them are a vegetable, similar to long green beans, but often a foot long – they are now available in the West in some Indian stores. They are often an ingredient of sambar (see p. 122) or are enjoyed in their own right, as here. The flavor is quite close to that of asparagus – but they grow on trees native to south India (the trees have tasty, edible leaves that resemble spinach in flavor).

Most drumsticks will need to have the stringy parts of their skins removed before cooking.

The best way to eat this dish is by picking up the drumstick pieces as if they were asparagus, eating the best bits and discarding anything tough.

1. Infuse the tamarind in ¼ cup of hot water for 5 minutes. Strain and put the liquid aside.

2. Wash the drumsticks. Trim them. Cut them into 3-inch lengths. Destring with a sharp knife if necessary. Boil them in a few tablespoons of water until tender.

3. Peel and chop the onion. Peel and crush the ginger and the garlic. Roughly chop the tomatoes.

4. In a saucepan melt 1 teaspoon of ghee and fry the onion and the mustard seeds together. When the mustard seeds pop, add the crushed ginger and garlic. Add the tomatoes and turmeric. Fry, uncovered, over a low heat until the mixture is simmering.

5. Add the drumsticks and brown sugar, salt to taste, and mix well. Cover the pan, reduce the heat and cook until the drumsticks are slightly brown, then add the strained tamarind juice.

6. Cover and cook over low heat until the drumsticks are soft (about 15–20 minutes).

Serrated gourd with shrimp

PEDUCHERRI PERKANKAI

2–3 serrated gourds (about
1 pound in weight)

1 medium onion

ghee

¼ cup shelled cooked shrimp

1 teaspoon black mustard seeds

This is one of my favorite vegetables – not only because it is one of the easiest vegetables to prepare, but because of its sweet and delicate flavor. As its name implies, the serrated gourd is a squash with ridged, rough skin, but is tender inside. This pale green vegetable is available from Indian and Chinese supermarkets.

Tamil women are said to resemble the serrated gourd – slightly sharp with strangers, yet soft and sweet with their loved ones!

With the shrimp, this dish is a wonderful combination of textures and flavors, of lusciousness and delicacy.

1. Wash the gourds, then peel away the hard, ridged parts of the skin, leaving the softer strips intact. Slice into rings about ⅛ inch thick. Peel the onion and chop coarsely.

2. In 1 teaspoon of ghee fry the onions until soft but not brown. Add the black mustard seeds. When they pop add the shrimp and fry for 2–5 minutes, depending on their size.

3. Finally add the sliced gourd, cover the pan and cook for a further 5 minutes. Serve hot.

Crisp-fried bitter gourd

BANDAPUR PARVAKAI

This dish lives up to its name, the orange flesh of the bitter gourd being very bitter indeed, and definitely an acquired taste. Tamilian men generally prefer the bitter gourd to the sweeter, serrated gourd preferred by women. However, since Tamilians believe that you should not end the day with bitterness – and this includes food – this

2–3 bitter gourds

½ teaspoon chili powder

salt to taste

1 teaspoon sugar

oil for frying

dish is never eaten at night. Bitter gourd is available from Indian shops (its Hindi name is kareli).

1. Wash the gourds and cut into ¼-inch slices. Cover them evenly with the chili powder, salt and sugar and leave to marinate for at least 30 minutes.

2. Heat 2 teaspoons of oil and fry the gourds, a few at a time, until crisp (about 5 minutes). Drain on paper towel and serve hot.

Zucchini in tamarind

CHIDDAMBARAM AMBAT

3–4 small zucchini

1½ medium onions

1 or 2 tomatoes

1 teaspoon tamarind

ghee for frying

1 teaspoon chili powder

½ teaspoon turmeric

salt to taste

1 teaspoon freshly ground black pepper

1 teaspoon black mustard seeds

Small zucchini picked early in the season are best for this dish, being sweeter, and their flavor is enhanced by the slight tartness of the tamarind.

1. Wash and peel the zucchini, then cut them into 1-inch cubes. Peel and slice the onions. Wash and chop the tomatoes.

2. Infuse the tamarind in ½ cup of boiling water for 5 minutes. Strain, and put the liquid to one side.

3. Heat 1 tablespoon of ghee and fry the onions until soft. Add the chili powder, turmeric, salt, black pepper and mustard seeds. Fry for 5 minutes or until browned and the mustard seeds have popped. Then add the tomatoes and diced zucchini. Cover and cook over a low heat for 10 minutes, shaking the pan from time to time.

4. Add the tamarind liquid. Continue to cook, uncovered, until the zucchini is nearly dry, then serve.

Broccoli with dried shrimp

RAMESWARAM KARAMANA UPKARI

2 ounces dried shrimp

1 pound broccoli

4 shallots

1 dried red chili

2 fresh green chilies

peanut oil

¼ teaspoon salt (or to taste)

1 teaspoon black mustard seeds

This is one of the dishes individual Tamil women have varied in their own ways over the centuries, making use of different green vegetables. It can also be made with spring greens, leeks, or fresh fava beans. Broccoli is unavailable in Madras, but I have chosen it for my variation of the dish as it combines so well with the shrimp. The chili adds a little extra interest. This is an excellent accompaniment to a simple meat or fish dish. Dried shrimp is available from Indian and Chinese stores.

1. Wash the dried shrimp. Leave to drain.

2. Cut the broccoli into small florets.

3. Peel and quarter the shallots. Deseed and slice the fresh green chilies. Cut the dried red chili into quarters.

4. Grind or finely chop the shallots, dried red chili and fresh green chilies in a food processor (or chop very finely, then grind in a mortar and pestle).

5. Heat 2 teaspoons of oil in a wok. Add the mustard seeds and fry until they pop. Then add the shallot mixture and dried shrimp, and fry until an aroma arises. Finally add the broccoli florets and 1 tablespoon of water, cover the pan and simmer for 8–10 minutes or until the broccoli is just softened and the shrimp is crisp.

Madras spinach

PALANKA KEERAI USAL

Many Tamil women subsidize the family income to help pay for a good education for their children – they grow leafy vegetables around their homes and sell their wares by carrying them in woven baskets on their heads around Madras.

1 pound spinach

1 medium onion

ghee

1 teaspoon black mustard seeds

salt to taste

Spinach grows well in Madras. It is a versatile vegetable that goes well with just about everything. This recipe is mild, and very simple and quick to prepare.

1. Wash the spinach and drain thoroughly. Remove any tough stalks and cut or tear the leaves into ½-inch strips. Peel and chop the onion.

2. Melt 1 teaspoon of ghee over a low heat and fry the onions until soft.

3. Add the black mustard seeds. When they pop add the spinach. Salt to taste. Cover and cook for about 2–3 minutes, until the spinach is soft but still bright green.

Cabbage with mustard seeds and onion

PALASANI ZUNAKA

¼ head firm white cabbage

1 medium onion

1 green chili

1 tablespoon mustard seeds

salt to taste

oil

The enormous, crisp and hard white cabbage, grown in the Ootacamund area are popular with housewives in Madras, being full of flavor as well as economical. Cabbage cooked according to this simple recipe is delicious, and retains some of its crisp texture. The mustard seeds add a little sweetness. It is ideal when served with a more powerful or fiery dish.

1. Wash the cabbage and slice it thinly.

2. Peel the onion, halve it and slice thinly into half-rings. Deseed and finely slice the green chili.

3. Fry the onion in 1 tablespoon of oil until soft but not browned. Add the mustard seeds and cook until they pop.

4. Add the chili and cabbage, with 1 tablespoon of water and salt.

5. Cover the pan and cook for about 6 minutes, or until the cabbage is just soft. Serve hot.

Bean sprouts and celery with cockles

PORT BLAIR ISTHAMANA KAI KOOTU

1 clove garlic

2–3 green chilies

1 red onion

1 stalk celery

½ pound bean sprouts

¼ pound fresh cockles, in shells

peanut oil

1 teaspoon black mustard seeds

salt to taste

This delicious vegetable dish with a taste of the sea comes from the Andaman Islands, where seafood is fresh and plentiful. When my grandfather (who was a chaplain in the army and was stationed for a while in the Andaman Islands) invited British officers and soldiers to a meal of cockles, mussels and shrimp, they would entertain him in turn by singing the well-known song "Molly Malone": "cockles and mussels alive alive-o!" This is a simple dish to prepare: fresh cockles will give the best results, though canned or bottled cockles can also be used.

1. Peel and crush the garlic. Deseed and slice the chilies. Peel and slice the onion. Slice the celery finely.

2. Rinse the bean sprouts and leave to drain thoroughly.

3. Prepare the cockles: wash them, then place in a bowl and cover with boiling water. Leave for 5 minutes, then drain. Pry open the shells and scoop out the cockles. Set to one side.

4. Heat 2 teaspoons of oil in a wok or frying pan and fry the crushed garlic until brown. Add the black mustard seeds and cook until they pop. Add the sliced onion and fresh red chilies and fry until soft and the onion has browned.

5. Then add the bean sprouts and celery and fry for a minute before adding the fresh cockles. Lower the heat, cover and cook for 10 minutes, until the cockles and vegetables are just soft.

Pumpkin with fenugreek

CHEYNEMPET PUSNIKA

¼ pumpkin (½ pound)

¼ teaspoon turmeric

1 small onion

¼ inch fresh ginger

2 green chilies

sprig cilantro

garlic

½–1 teaspoon fenugreek seeds
(to taste)

oil for frying

¼ cup freshly grated coconut
(optional)

salt to taste

This dish is a glorious golden yellow, the color of the tiger, and the color of the necklace a woman wears as a symbol of marriage. This is my mother's recipe, which I loved as a child, in which the chilies add a little fire and the fenugreek a sweetish, but bitter note.

1. Prepare the pumpkin: scoop out the seeds and pith, then peel and cube the flesh. Parboil it with the turmeric until it begins to soften (5–8 minutes).

2. Peel the onion. Chop coarsely. Peel the ginger and chop roughly (or grate).

3. Deseed the chili, slice finely. Roughly chop the cilantro. Peel and chop the garlic.

4. Fry the fenugreek seeds in 2 teaspoons of oil. Then add the chopped onion, garlic and ginger. Cook until the onion softens.

5. Add the pumpkin (and coconut if you are using it) and salt to taste. Cover the pan and finish cooking over low heat for 5–10 minutes (stir in the cilantro toward the end of cooking). The ingredients will be golden yellow and the pumpkin soft enough to pierce easily with a fork.

Masala potato

KELANGA GHASHASHI

3 medium potatoes

1 cup water

2 medium onions

½ inch fresh ginger

4 cloves garlic

2 fresh green chilies

½ lime

1 teaspoon sesame seeds

1 teaspoon white poppy seeds
(see Glossary)

4 stalks cilantro

ghee

¼ teaspoon turmeric

½ teaspoon chili powder

2 teaspoons ground coriander

salt to taste

½ teaspoon cumin seeds

FACING PAGE: *Fried small purple eggplant (p. 42); charred sweet peppers (p. 41); tomato chutney (p. 118); spiced lentils,* dhall *(p. 62); masala potato (p. 56) and chappatis (p. 27)*

Tamilians are a friendly people and company is always welcome, especially during the religious festivals of Diwali, Pongal, Ramadan, Bakrid, Christmas and Easter. This recipe has been a popular one since my grandfather's time. As an army chaplain he was always entertaining British guests – officers and soldiers, as well as missionaries and members of their congregations. All the English visitors enjoyed masala potato, perhaps because it has both a touch of home and of the country they had come to call home. (The best potatoes for this recipe are fairly new, waxy ones.)

1. Wash the potatoes. Boil them (in their skins) in a saucepan of salted water until three-quarters done (time will depend on size). Drain, then peel and dice them.

2. Peel and slice finely the onions, ginger and garlic. Deseed and slice the chilies. Squeeze the juice of half a lime and set aside.

3. Heat a heavy-based pan and roast the sesame seeds and poppy seeds until golden – keep them on the move so they don't burn.

4. Grind the fresh green chilies, garlic, ginger and half the cilantro in a food processor. Set to one side.

5. Heat 2 teaspoons of ghee in a heavy-based saucepan. Fry the onions until soft. Then add the ground ingredients and keep frying over medium heat until an aroma arises.

6. Next stir in the turmeric, chili powder, ground coriander and salt to taste. Fry for another 2 minutes before adding the potatoes. Make sure the potatoes are well coated with the ingredients in the pan, then stir in the lime juice.

7. Cook uncovered for another 5 minutes and then add the roasted sesame and poppy seeds and the cumin seeds. Sauté for a further 5 minutes. Serve garnished with the remaining cilantro.

3. Heat 1 tablespoon of oil in a pan, and add the black mustard seeds. Cook until they pop, then add the fenugreek seeds and coriander seeds, and cook until they brown slightly.

4. Add the onion, green chili and turmeric, and fry until soft and brown. Pour in the tamarind juice and simmer for 5 minutes. Finally stir in the mashed potato and add salt to taste. Cover the pan and cook gently for a further 5 minutes. Serve hot.

Carrots with aniseed

COIMBATORE KOCHHOLI

4 medium tender, young carrots

2 medium onions

2 ripe tomatoes

1 teaspoon aniseed

ghee

1 teaspoon black mustard seeds

¼ teaspoon turmeric

½ teaspoon chili powder

1 teaspoon salt

fresh dill

cilantro

A Tamil housewife always has to be prepared, like the Boy Scouts. In many Tamilian homes it is always open house: a colleague, friend or relative who drops in unexpectedly is always invited to join the family dinner. A Tamil woman learns the art of making a meal stretch for unexpected visitors very early on, and as carrots are cheap, a housewife always keeps a few in her vegetable basket for such emergencies.

In this recipe the color of the carrots is enhanced with tomatoes, and the aniseed adds its own special flavor.

(This recipe also works well with parsnips; we have no parsnips in Madras, but they resemble a type of green carrot that is often prepared in this way.)

1. Peel and finely dice the carrots (¼-inch cubes). Peel and slice the onions coarsely. Quarter the tomatoes.

2. Lightly crush the aniseed in a mortar and pestle. Heat 2 teaspoons of ghee in a small wok or saucepan and add the mustard seeds and aniseed. When the mustard seeds pop add the onion and fry until golden brown.

3. Add the turmeric, chili powder and salt and fry for about 2 minutes. When an aroma arises, add the tomatoes. Lower the heat and cook, stirring frequently, until the tomatoes are soft. Add the carrots and 2 tablespoons of water. Cover the pan tightly and cook over a low heat until the carrots become tender (10–15 minutes). Serve garnished with the fresh dill and cilantro.

Malar's root vegetables in hot tamarind sauce

MALAR'S SUKKEE

5 shallots

2 cloves garlic

2 fresh red chilies

¼ rutabaga

1 medium carrot

1 small parsnip

3 small potatoes

2 tomatoes

1 tablespoon tamarind

2 teaspoons brown sugar

oil

¼ teaspoon turmeric

½ teaspoon chili powder

1 teaspoon ground coriander

salt to taste

This Tamilian dish, which uses root vegetables in a spicy but sweet tamarind sauce, gives very ordinary ingredients an unusual Tamilian flavor (in Madras, crimson yam is used, rather than rutabaga).

1. Peel the shallots and chop coarsely. Peel the garlic. Wash and deseed the fresh red chilies. Grind or mince the shallots, garlic and chilies together in a mortar and pestle or food processor. Set aside.

2. Peel the rutabaga, carrots, parsnip and potatoes. Quarter the tomatoes.

3. Infuse the tamarind in 1 cup of boiling water for 5 minutes and strain. Add the brown sugar, mix well and put to one side.

4. Heat 1 tablespoon of oil in a heavy-based saucepan and fry the ground onion mixture with the turmeric, chili powder, ground coriander, and salt. Stir in the prepared vegetables and coat them with the ground ingredients. Then add the tamarind juice and tomatoes. Bring to the boil. Lower the heat immediately, cover the pan and cook until all the vegetables are soft (15–20 minutes).

Spiced lentils

DHALL (THUVARAI PARPU)

1 clove garlic

1 medium onion

1 cup split red grams (shelled toor dhall) or red lentils (masoor dhall)

2 cups hot water

1 teaspoon salt (or to taste)

1 teaspoon turmeric

oil

1 teaspoon black mustard seeds

Dhall *(the Hindi word;* parpu *is Tamil) denotes not only the dry split peas or lentils but also a cooked preparation which, in its many varieties, is eaten all over the subcontinent. Dhall forms an important part of the diet, especially for vegetarians. A staple of the Brahmins, legumes, or grams, are considered a very pure food, and their purity is enhanced by the fact that they grow above ground, and are blown by the wind. Grams are an excellent source of protein, and are quite delicious – in India they are cooked with age-old skills that make them substantial yet fragrant. Split red grams (shelled toor dhall), which in this recipe need to be soaked for an hour before cooking, or red lentils (masoor dhall) can be used. The former are usually preferred in Tamil Nadu. Dhall is cooked to many consistencies varying from thick to quite liquid, according to taste – the quantities below will give a fairly thick consistency. [See Glossary for more about dhall.]*

Here the mustard seeds add a touch of sweetness; sweet red peppers could be added for more color.

1. If using toor dhall, soak in water for an hour before use.

2. Peel the garlic and slightly crush the clove with a pestle or the flat of a knife blade. Peel the onion and chop finely.

3. Wash the grams or lentils thoroughly and place in a large pan or pressure cooker with the hot water.

4. Add salt, turmeric and the crushed garlic. Bring to the boil.

5. Reduce the heat and simmer (half-covered, so the pan doesn't boil over) until the lentils are soft (10 minutes for red lentils, 30 minutes for toor dhall).

6. Fry the onion, over low heat, in 1 teaspoon of oil until soft and brown. Add the mustard seeds and cook until they pop.

7. Add the onions to the soft lentils and cook for a further 5–10 minutes.

Indians are proud of their national identity, and the colors of the Indian national flag can be seen in an average Indian meal; orange in parpu, green in a leafy vegetable and white in rice.

Nilgiris salad

NILGIRIS PACHADI

1 medium carrot

½ head crisp white cabbage

1 small onion

½ sweet red pepper

½ green pepper

½ cucumber

4–5 green grapes

4–5 black grapes

6–7 strawberries, when available

2 peaches

2 tangerines

1 small apple

1 tablespoon sunflower seeds

2 tablespoons chopped walnuts

2 firm tomatoes

¼ cup plain yogurt

1 sprig cilantro

Salads are not a traditional part of Tamil cuisine, so there are no specific Tamilian recipes. However, salads have been a favorite in my family since the days of my grandfather, who traveled to England at a time when few Tamilians went there. According to family legend, he loved a good salad! I have created this delicious and colorful dish of fruit, nuts and vegetables – with its own special blend of yogurt and cilantro to give it a Tamilian touch – and have named it after the beautiful Nilgiri hills. I serve it with biryani (p. 20) on special occasions, and it always proves a popular complement to the richness of the biryani. The crunchiness of the nuts and sunflower seeds makes a delightful contrast to the juicy fruit and crisp vegetables.

1. Grate the carrot finely. Finely slice the cabbage and onion.

2. Cut the red and green peppers and cucumber into small cubes.

3. Halve the grapes and strawberries. Peel and slice the peaches.

4. Quarter the segments of the tangerines. Peel and slice the apple.

5. Place all the above ingredients in a bowl and add the sunflower seeds and walnuts. Gently stir in the yogurt and add the chopped cilantro.

FISH AND SEAFOOD

Many Tamilians look to the sea for their livelihood, as they did in ages past, and it is wonderful to hear fishermen chanting ancient songs of the sea as they row their boats along the shore. Tamilians have a rich profusion of fresh fish and seafood right at their doorstep, both from the seas that wash the coasts and from the five large, well-stocked rivers. Fish from Madras is now exported all over the world and is an important part of the Madras economy.

Fish is considered a food "for the brain," and is eaten by all, including some Brahmins, whose diet is otherwise vegetarian.

The wealth of seafood includes delicious crabs – the small blue-colored crabs are from the sea, and the large black crabs are freshwater – packed with firm, sweet flesh; there are juicy cockles, mussels and other shellfish; plump shrimp (large, blue-veined, tiger and pink) and glorious lobsters. Among the fish are Spanish mackerel, pomfret, grouper, Malabar sole, whitebait, pilchards, shark and swordfish. In the city of Madras you can go down to the Marina shore, one of the longest beaches in the world, to buy tiger shrimp and fish straight from the fishermen's boats.

FACING PAGE: *Marina shrimp (p. 67), drumsticks (p. 49) and rice with fresh lime (p. 15)*

Masala lobsters

MAMMALAPURAM KAL ERRA

1–2 fresh lobsters (1 pound), boiled

1 inch fresh ginger

2 fresh green chilies

4 teaspoons black mustard seeds

¼ teaspoon turmeric

½ teaspoon chili powder

salt to taste

1 teaspoon aniseed

1 teaspoon fenugreek seeds

1 teaspoon cumin seeds

vegetable oil

2 tender banana leaves or sprig of cilantro and foil

Baked lobster with spices, wrapped in banana leaves, and baked in smoldering coals is delicious. If banana leaves cannot be found, foil will do – you will still achieve a mouth-watering result! The lobsters can be cooked over a cooling barbecue, or in an oven.

1. Remove the lobster from the shell: remove the head and tail, pry the lobster shell away from the flesh.

2. Peel and slice the ginger. Deseed and slice the fresh chilies. Grind 3 teaspoons of the mustard seeds, ginger and chili to a very fine paste in a mortar and pestle, or in the small bowl of a food processor. Place in a bowl and add turmeric, chili powder and salt.

3. In a coffee grinder, or mortar and pestle, grind together the aniseed, fenugreek, cumin and remaining teaspoon of mustard seeds.

4. Heat 1 tablespoon of oil and add the ground seeds. Fry briefly, pour over the ginger and chili paste, and mix well.

5. Liberally coat the lobsters with this paste, wrap in banana leaves (or wrap, together with a sprig of cilantro, in foil). Place on a baking tray and bake in a moderately hot oven (375°F), or in the coals of a barbecue, for 20–30 minutes, depending on size. Serve.

FACING PAGE: *Serrated gourd with shrimp (p. 50), fish in tamarind sauce (p. 75) and simple rice (p. 14)*

This is a very special dish, which often forms part of the meal of the bridal party the night before a wedding. There is much laughter, teasing and a few tears throughout the day among the bride and her happy young sisters and friends. In the evening the mother offers prayers in the home, followed by a feast of deliciously prepared dishes, such as this, which they all share.

Madurai mussels

MADURAI KILANJAL

2 pounds mussels, in shells

½ teaspoon turmeric

3 fresh red chilies

1 inch fresh ginger

3 cloves garlic

2 whole cloves

1 tablespoon tamarind

3 small onions

peanut oil

1 teaspoon fenugreek seeds

½ cup thin coconut milk (see Glossary)

salt

The ancient city of Madurai was home to the Pandya kings over a thousand years ago. They built some of most dramatic gopurams *in Tamil Nadu, soaring Hindu temples with exquisite carving.*

The combination of spices and coconut in this recipe bring out the full flavor of the sea-fresh mussels, making a fragrant sauce. Mussels, eaten with the fingers in Madras, are served with rice. (The mussel shells are rubbed with spices that can sting – it is best to wear rubber gloves.) Remember to discard any mussels that do not rise to the surface of a bowl of water.

1. Scrub the mussels; remove the beards. Rub turmeric over the shells; set aside.

2. Deseed two of the fresh red chilies, chop finely. Peel and slice the ginger and garlic. Grind the chopped red chilies, cloves, garlic and ginger to a fine paste in a mortar and pestle, or food processor with a small bowl. Wearing rubber gloves, rub the paste over the turmeric-covered mussel shells; set aside for an hour.

3. Infuse the tamarind in ¼ cup of hot water for 5 minutes. Strain and set the liquid to one side. Peel the onions; chop finely.

4. Heat 1 tablespoon of oil in a large saucepan or wok over medium heat. Fry the fenugreek seeds until golden brown. Then add half the chopped onion and cook until brown and soft. Put in the marinated mussels and continue to fry for 5–6 minutes, stirring occasionally. Lower the heat.

5. Stir in the coconut milk and tamarind liquid. Add salt to taste. Then add the remaining onions. Mix well. Cover and cook for 5–10 minutes, stirring occasionally. When the shells begin to open, taste and add more salt if necessary. Once the shells are open, the mussels are cooked.

6. Place the mussels in a large serving bowl (discard any that have not opened). Garnish with the remaining red chili.

Fish in tamarind sauce

RUNGASWAMY MEEN KOLOMBA

2 whole mackerel, mullet or trout, or 1 pound monkfish, cod, or other firm-fleshed fish

salt

2 teaspoons chili powder

1 tablespoon ground coriander

1¼ tablespoons tamarind

1 medium onion

2 cloves garlic

2 tomatoes

oil

1 tablespoon fenugreek seeds

1 teaspoon tomato paste

1 tablespoon cilantro

This delicious masterpiece improves by being kept overnight to allow the fish to absorb the flavor of the sauce (it is quickly reheated). As the tamarind is acidic, it's best to avoid an aluminum pot – traditionally this is made in a clay pot, but stainless steel is often used today.

1. Scale and clean the fish thoroughly. Wash and dry the fish and sprinkle with a little salt. Cut whole fish into 3 or 4 pieces or fillets into pieces about 2 x 3 inches.

2. Make a paste with the chili powder, ground coriander and 1 tablespoon of hot water.

3. Infuse the tamarind in 1½ cups of boiling water for 5 minutes, then strain and reserve the liquid.

4. Peel the onion and chop coarsely. Peel the garlic, chop finely. Roughly chop the tomatoes.

5. Fry the garlic and onions in oil until soft. Add the fenugreek seeds and fry them until the aroma is released.

6. Add the chili and ground coriander paste. Fry for 2 minutes. Then slowly add the tamarind liquid while stirring. Bring to the boil.

7. Add the tomatoes and tomato paste.

8. Boil for about 15 minutes before adding the fish. Lower the heat, cover the pan and simmer for about 10 minutes. Just at the end of cooking add the cilantro.

Bright sunshine throughout the day makes it possible for housewives to leave the kitchen doors wide open and do some kitchen work outside: there is always a space for grinding, for cleaning fish, for scouring pots and pans with a coconut husk. Here, the heavy grinding granite stone and the heavy mortar and pestle have pride of place. Until recently, many Tamilians would employ a servant to help with heavy tasks, as labor used to be cheap. Times are changing in modern Madras, however, and labor-saving devices such as food processors and modern stoves mean that many people now manage without extra help.

Monkfish in coconut

MEEN MOLI

Meen is Tamil for fish, and moli (a name given by the English mem-sahibs) the sauce – with its wonderful combination of coconut, green chilies and ginger. Anyone who loves fish should try this delicious sweet-yet-fiery dish. Meen moli is a speciality of the restaurants in the ancient city of Madurai, home of many temple festivals, and is enjoyed all along the coast of south India.

1 pound monkfish (or other firm-fleshed fish such as cod, halibut or mullet)

½ teaspoon salt (or to taste)

1 teaspoon turmeric

3 medium onions

4–5 cloves of garlic

1 inch fresh ginger

3 fresh green chilies

half a lemon

2 tomatoes

ghee

¾ cup thin coconut milk

½ cup thick coconut milk (see Glossary)

1 teaspoon brown sugar

1. Clean or skin the fish as required, and cut into pieces about 2 inches square. Sprinkle evenly with the salt and turmeric. Marinate for half an hour.

2. Peel the onions. Quarter one of them.

3. Peel the garlic and ginger. Deseed the fresh green chilies. Place the garlic, ginger and chilies in a food processor with the quartered onion, and grind to a fine pulp (not a purée). Or chop very finely and grind in a mortar and pestle.

4. Quarter the remaining onions, then slice finely. Crush them slightly (to help them soften when cooking) in a mortar and pestle or with a rolling pin.

5. Squeeze the juice of half a lemon. Roughly chop the tomatoes.

6. Heat 1 tablespoon of ghee in a frying pan and fry the fish just long enough to seal it. Set it aside. In another pan heat 1 tablespoon of ghee over a low heat, and fry the finely ground onion mixture. When the aroma is released, add the thin coconut milk and the chopped tomatoes. Bring it to the boil. Then add the fish and the finely sliced onions and cook for another 5 minutes. Lower the heat and let it simmer slowly for 5–10 minutes (depending on how quickly the fish is cooking).

7. Add the lemon juice, thick coconut milk, sugar and salt to taste. Simmer for a further 1–2 minutes. (The fish should be cooked and the sauce should have a creamy, pouring consistency.) Remove from the heat and serve.

FACING PAGE: *Monkfish in coconut, pumpkin with fenugreek (p. 55), snow peas with ginger and chili (p. 43) and tomato rice (p. 19)*

Fish baked in banana leaves

ENAPPA CHUTTA VANJARAM

1 small onion

2 fresh green chilies

2 teaspoons black mustard seeds

2 teaspoons brown sugar

1 pound mullet or mackerel, filleted

salt to taste

½ teaspoon turmeric

1 teaspoon chili powder

¼ cup cornstarch

1 tablespoon mustard oil

1 teaspoon sesame oil

2 tender banana leaves

Here, mullet or mackerel are marinated in spices, wrapped in banana leaves and baked in hot ashes – ideal for when a summer barbecue is cooling. The banana leaves keep the fish moist and give it a unique and delightful, slightly fruity, flavor. In the absence of either banana leaves or barbecue, the fish can be wrapped in foil and oven-baked.

1. Peel and chop the onion. Deseed and slice the fresh green chilies. Grind together the onion, chilies, mustard seeds and sugar in a food processor (or chop finely and grind in a mortar and pestle). Remove and set aside.

2. Wash and dry the fish. Cut into 2-inch squares. Sprinkle evenly with salt, turmeric and chili powder. Mix the ground onion mixture with the cornstarch, mustard oil and sesame oil, and rub over the fish. Leave the fish to marinate for at least half an hour.

3. Cut the banana leaves into eight pieces (cut lengthwise, then across to make quarters, then halve the quarters). Wash and dry the pieces.

4. Roll a strip of fish in a piece of banana leaf or foil (seal the banana leaf with ghee). Fold over both ends.

5. Bake on a cooling barbecue, or in a moderate oven (350°F) for 10–15 minutes (or until the fish is tender).

Banana leaves have many uses. Being clean and moist, they make a good wrapper for fish or meat bought in the market, and, cut into squares, they serve as excellent plates. As they are used only once, they are always considered pure. At the end of a meal each person folds the leaf over, towards himeslf or herself, to express gratitude for a meal well served.

Spicy whitebait

APPA ODAI NETHALI

½ tablespoon tamarind

1 pound whitebait

1 medium-sized onion

2 fresh green chilies

ghee

1 teaspoon fenugreek seeds

1 teaspoon tomato paste

salt to taste

This recipe has been in our family for several generations. It was a dish my father particularly liked for its sweetness and delicate spices, and my mother was given the recipe by my paternal grandmother. Whitebait are fragile and you need to treat them gently in cooking to prevent them breaking up.

1. Infuse the tamarind in 2 tablespoons of hot water for 5 minutes. Strain and set aside.

2. Wash the whitebait.

3. Peel the onion and chop coarsely. Deseed and slice the green chilies. Blend the onions and chilies together in a food processor until a smooth paste is obtained.

4. Heat 2 tablespoons of ghee in a medium-sized saucepan over medium heat. Fry the fenugreek seeds until brown. Add the onion and chili paste. Next add the tamarind liquid, tomato paste and salt to taste, and bring it to the boil. Finally add the whitebait with 2 teaspoons of cold water. Stir gently and cook for 2 minutes. Shake the saucepan gently to prevent sticking. Remove from the heat and serve with rice and vegetables.

The time when a young Tamil girl reaches maturity is special and Tamilians mark this occasion with a celebration. The young maiden is dressed like one of the famous Meenakshi dolls, in her best sari. Her hair is adorned with flowers and the young maiden sits on a coconut leaf in her room.

According to this ancient custom, this was the time she was viewed as a marriage partner for a lucky young man. For two weeks she is treated like a queen. Special fish dishes are prepared to tempt her appetite. Meenakshi, the Goddess of the Sea, looks down kindly on this young maiden.

MEAT AND POULTRY

These dominions are provided with quantities of cattle such as cows and sheep, also of birds both those belonging to the hills and those recorded at home and those in greater abundance than in our tracts. They give three fowls in the city for a coin worth a vintem, outside the city they give five fowls for a vintem. In the country there are many ducks. All these birds are very cheap. The sheep they kill every day are countless, one could not count them, for in every street there are men who will sell you mutton so clean and so fat that it looks like beef; and you also have pigs in some streets of butcher's houses so black and clean that you could never see better in any country.

<small>Don Pasquales (a Portuguese merchant and traveler who lived in Viyayanagar for many years), 1587.</small>

Generally, meat is marinated in spices before cooking – often for just half an hour. Yet meat for some recipes is marinated overnight so the aromatics have more chance to penetrate and tenderize it. A little water is added to the spices when marinating meat, to keep it moist – yogurt is also sometimes used as it tenderizes the meat and helps to thicken the final sauce. It also helps the flavor to penetrate the meat by carrying the aromatics inside the fibers. (Where meat needs to be marinated for a long period, or overnight, this is noted at the start of the recipe.)

The main spices used to marinate meat are chili powder and turmeric. Ground cumin with chili is preferred in cooking lamb, along with cinnamon stick, cloves and cardamom, while ground coriander is used with chicken, beef and pork. In the recipes in this book, I have kept the combinations of spices simple, since I was taught that the aroma and flavor of natural ingredients should be enhanced and not smothered. As my grandmother used to say: "A neighbor should be able to tell what is cooking." Overspicing is never good cooking, and many dishes need only the merest suspicion of aromatics.

Until chili was brought to India from South America, the main "hot" spice was the peppercorn. *Thallitakari*, or just *kari,* is the term used for meat cooked with peppercorns, and is the origin of the word "curry."

The secret of braising meat lies in stewing it until it is saturated with the flavor of the aromatics. It is usually cooked in bite-sized pieces, except in biryanis and pulaos where bigger pieces are required. For tougher meats, a long slow simmering is sometimes required to extract the juices; this softens the fibers and results in the meat being extremely tender.

Meat is prepared in various ways, with or without sauce. Vegetables such as potatoes, carrots, turnips, green beans, snow peas, peppers and mushrooms are added to some meat dishes to add texture and flavor.

Sauces are derived from coconut milk – sweet and delicately flavored; from tamarind juices – acidic and sweet; or yogurt – rich and mild. Coconut milk added to sauces while cooking helps reduce their fieriness. Tomatoes and tomato paste are added but must be used with caution and subtlety, as they can mask the flavor and aroma of aromatics and spices. The thickness of a spicy sauce depends both on the cooking method used and the length of time that meat and onions are browned. Browned onions are an important thickener, and sauces are never thickened with flour.

Meat is served as a side dish only, unlike in the West where it forms the main part of the meal accompanied by vegetables. Some sections of the Tamil community don't eat certain types of meat for religious reasons: Hindus don't eat beef (the Brahmin caste is completely vegetarian), while pork is taboo to Muslims. Christians (who form the second largest religious community in Madras) and Muslims both eat beef, though, and the smaller communities of Anglo-Indians and Chinese sometimes enjoy the wild boar, whose flesh is sweeter than that of the domestic pig. Nearly all Tamilians eat mutton, lamb and chicken.

Lamb, being fatty but tender, is ideal for pulaos, biryanis and barbecues. Shoulder, leg slices and neck fillets are ideal for lamb cooked in spicy sauces. For my beef dishes I use T-bone, porterhouse or sirloin; when choosing a cut of pork I use the leg, as it has a mixture of white and dark meat.

Meat is still sold in every street from little huts in the mornings only — and the butcher's only implement is a wooden board and a sharp knife which cuts and minces very effectively. The meat is then wrapped in banana leaves and sold to the customers. Fresh chickens are sold in an adjoining hut — some are sold, live, in the markets.

Kotogari chicken

KOTOGARI KARAGU

½ pound chicken breasts (thighs may be used instead)

1 teaspoon chili powder

½ teaspoon turmeric

1 medium onion

¼ inch fresh ginger

1–2 cloves of garlic

1 large tomato

oil

1 tablespoon ground coriander

salt and pepper to taste

1 teaspoon tomato paste

juice of ½ lime

Kotogari is a town in the hills, popular with visitors to Madras as a refuge from the summer heat. My mother made this beautifully spiced chicken dish for friends of mine when they visited ten years ago, and they talk of it still. It is simple to make, and a favorite in the classes I teach. Made without the chili powder it is still delicious, but the turmeric (the true spice of south India) is essential.

1. Cut the chicken into portions about 2 inches square. Wash them and season with the chili powder and turmeric. Set aside.

2. Peel the onion and slice into thin rings. Peel, then chop or grate the ginger and garlic. Slice the tomato.

3. Fry the onion rings in 1 tablespoon of oil until soft and medium brown.

4. Add the chicken pieces and fry quite fast to brown the chicken. Add the garlic and ginger, ground coriander, and the salt and pepper.

5. Finally add the tomato, tomato paste and lime juice. Finish cooking over a low heat until the chicken is cooked (10–15 minutes). Serve hot.

LEFT: *Carrying poultry to market*

FACING PAGE: *Kotogari chicken, Madras spinach (p.52), decorated rice (p. 15) with plain yogurt*

Chicken kurma

KOLI KURMA

1 pound chicken breasts or thighs

½ teaspoon chili powder

¼ teaspoon turmeric

1 teaspoon salt

¼ cup plain yogurt

1 medium onion

1 green chili

2 cloves garlic

¼ inch fresh ginger

oil

small piece asafetida (size of a black peppercorn)

¼ inch cinnamon stick

1 medium tomato

1 tablespoon ground coriander

2 teaspoons ground cumin

1 teaspoon tomato paste

1 cup thick coconut milk (see Glossary)

Optional: ¼ cup ground almonds; stalk of cilantro

Koor means sharp, but kurma *is quite the opposite – a mild dish especially recommended to anyone wary of Tamilian spices. Kurma, or korma, is a dish of meat in a mild and creamy sauce, prepared all over India. In the north it betrays its Persian influence as the meat is braised with yogurt and cream, whereas the creaminess in the Tamilian version comes from coconut (a richer sauce is made by the optional addition of ground almonds).*

1. Wash and dry the chicken (remove the skin if preferred). Season the chicken with the chili powder, turmeric, salt and plain yogurt. Leave for at least 1 hour.

2. Peel the onion, then quarter it. Deseed the green chili. Then grind the onion and chili to a paste in a food processor, or chop finely and grind with a mortar and pestle.

3. Peel the garlic and ginger, chop finely and grind to a coarse paste with a mortar and pestle.

4. In 1 tablespoon of oil fry the asafetida and piece of cinnamon stick. When there is an aroma add the onion and chili mixture and fry until soft.

5. Add the marinated chicken pieces and fry gently for 10 minutes. Quarter the tomato. When the chicken is brown add the garlic and ginger paste together with the ground coriander and cumin, the tomato and tomato paste.

6. Continue to fry for about 5 minutes. Slowly add ¼ cup of water and the coconut milk, and stir to make a sauce.

7. Cover and finish cooking over a low heat for 20–30 minutes or until the chicken is ready. The ground almonds may be stirred in towards the end, to make a richer sauce. Chop the cilantro and stir in at the end of cooking.

Fried spicy chicken

KOZHI SHULLI

4–6 chicken breasts

1 teaspoon chili powder

¼ teaspoon turmeric

½ teaspoon salt (or to taste)

oil

These delicious morsels of fried chicken are an ideal appetizer, giving guests a spicy taste of things to come. They are best accompanied by other items to nibble, such as slices of raw cucumber or carrot, shredded fresh coconut and roasted peanuts.

1. Wash and dry the chicken breasts, remove the skin, and cut into strips about 1 inch across. Evenly cover the chicken strips with the chili, turmeric and salt, and marinate for at least an hour.

2. Heat 2–3 tablespoons of oil in a frying pan, and fry the chicken strips a few at a time until golden brown (about 5 minutes). Drain on paper towel and serve right away.

Some Tamil girls who have marriages arranged for them do not enjoy any courting and wooing. On her wedding night her husband starts their married life by courting the bride. The bridal couple are usually left a plate of small titbits and snacks on a table beside their bed, which is decorated with strings of jasmine. The bride is escorted to the bedroom by her mother, sisters and friends, all giving advice in between girlish laughter.

The husband soon follows, and tempts his shy bride with the delicious fare . . .

Tandoori chicken

RANI SUNTHAKAS

4–6 chicken thighs

1 teaspoon chili powder

¼ teaspoon turmeric

1 small onion

¼ inch fresh ginger

2 cloves garlic

6 cardamom pods

1 teaspoon raisins

juice of ½ lime

1 tablespoon tandoori powder

1 tablespoon plain yogurt

1 teaspoon ground coriander

½ teaspoon salt (or to taste)

peanut oil

Traditionally most cooking in India is done in pans, over heat. In addition tandoors, or clay ovens, have been used from earliest times, and they give a good, dry heat. Foods cooked in these ovens retain their pure, unique flavors. However, you can use an oven at a high temperature to achieve the tandoor effect. Chicken tandoori has become a favorite in Britain and North America, generally cooked northern-style. In Madras we have our own version, with onion, garlic, ginger and raisins added to the masala paste. To save time, use bought tandoori powder instead of the masala (spice blend).

Tomato chutney (see p. 118) makes a good accompaniment, with rice.

◆ The meat needs to be marinated for at least 4 hours before cooking.

1. Wash and dry the chicken, remove the skin if preferred. Cover evenly with the chili and turmeric.

2. Peel the onion and quarter it. Peel the ginger and garlic. Remove cardamom seeds from the pods, discard pods. Place in a food processor with the raisins, and grind to a paste (or chop finely and pound them with a mortar and pestle).

3. Mix the masala or bought tandoori powder to a paste with the yogurt and 2 teaspoons of lime juice.

4. Cut slits in the chicken, then coat evenly with the masala or tandoori paste, ground coriander, salt and the ground onion and spice mixture. Leave for 4 hours.

5. Preheat the oven on maximum heat. Reduce the heat of the oven to 350°F, place the chicken pieces on a greased tray and roast for 1 hour (turn the chicken pieces and brush with a little oil halfway through cooking).

A 3rd-century poem, the Perampanuru, *tells of a traveler being served white rice and the flesh of a fowl roasted in spices by his host, a farmer – this must surely be the first written description of tandoori chicken.*

Barbecued chicken on skewers

TUTUKORI THANDURAM

MAKES 10 "KEBABS"

1 small onion

3 cloves garlic

1 inch fresh ginger

1 teaspoon white poppy seeds
(see Glossary)

1 teaspoon lovage seeds

¼ inch cinnamon stick

2 teaspoons ground coriander

1 teaspoon chili powder

white vinegar

sesame oil

½ cup plain yogurt

salt

1 teaspoon brown sugar

1 teaspoon freshly ground black
pepper

juice of a lime

1 pound chicken thighs or breasts

20 shallots

10 cherry tomatoes

1 green pepper

1 sweet red pepper

1 teaspoon red food coloring

Tamilians, especially young people, love barbecues – I certainly did in my student days. Traditionally, cooking over fire was thought to purify food.

This dish is equally well suited to the long hot days of summer: pieces of spiced chicken are threaded onto skewers with marinated shallots and cherry tomatoes, and with sweet peppers, then grilled.

◆ The chicken needs to be marinated for at least 4 hours before cooking (the longer the better) and the vegetables for 2 hours.

1. Peel the small onion and quarter it. Peel the garlic and ginger. Place in a food processor with the poppy seeds, lovage seeds and cinnamon stick, and chop to a smooth consistency (or chop finely and pound with a mortar and pestle).

2. Add the ground coriander, chili powder, 2 teaspoons of vinegar, 1 tablespoon of sesame oil, yogurt, 1 teaspoon of salt, sugar, pepper and coloring. Add half the lime juice (reserve the remainder).

3. Cut the chicken into around 20 cubes and mix with the paste, making sure all the pieces are well coated. Set aside for 4–8 hours.

4. Meanwhile peel the shallots. Wash the cherry tomatoes. Mix the remaining lime juice with 1 teaspoon of vinegar, ½ teaspoon of salt and 1 tablespoon of sesame oil. Marinate the tomatoes and shallots in this mixture for 2 hours.

5. Wash the peppers and cut each into 10 pieces.

6. Thread 10 skewers, each with 1 tomato, 2 shallots, 1 piece of each pepper and 2 pieces of chicken. Grill, turning frequently, until the chicken is cooked (3 minutes on a hot barbecue, 5 minutes under a hot broiler). Drizzle with oil if they appear to be drying out.

Roast marinated chicken

KARUGU BHARJANAM

1 small chicken (2–2½ pounds)

1 inch fresh ginger

2 cloves garlic

2 fresh red chilies

2 cardamom pods

2 whole cloves

handful cilantro

¼ inch cinnamon stick

¼ cup plain yogurt

1 medium red onion

Tamilian women have put their own special touches to dishes they have enjoyed in other parts of the world, for they carry their palettes of spices with them, as artists carry their colors.

This is my own recipe for roast chicken, flavored with the spices of my homeland – bharjanam means to roast. The sliced onions add sweetness, and make an attractive garnish. I serve it with masala potato (p. 56), tomato or eggplant chutney (pp. 117, 118) and snow peas with ginger and chili (p. 43).

◆ The marinating should be started 4 or 5 hours before cooking, so that the yogurt can tenderize the meat.

1. Wash and dry the chicken, inside and out.

2. Peel and roughly chop the fresh ginger and garlic. Deseed the fresh red chilies. Open the cardamom pods and remove the seeds, discarding the pods.

3. Finely chop the ginger, garlic, chili, cardamom seeds, cloves, cilantro and cinnamon stick and grind with a mortar and pestle (or grind together in a food processor that has a bowl for small quantities).

4. Place in a dish large enough to hold the chicken, and add the yogurt. Stir it well. Place the chicken in the dish and turn it in the mixture until evenly covered. Marinate for 4–5 hours.

5. Peel the onion and slice into rings ¼ inch thick.

6. Prepare the oven: the chicken will go on a roasting rack (or directly on the shelf) with a tray beneath it. Preheat to 325°F.

7. Remove the chicken from the marinade. Place the chicken on the rack and cover with the onion slices. Pour ¼ cup of water into the tray (this will help crisp the skin). Roast for 1½ hours or until the chicken is cooked.

Duck with coconut

VEDDUVAR VARTHA

1 3-pound duck (or 1 pound duck breasts)

salt to taste

2 medium onions

4 fresh red chilies

2 cloves garlic

½ inch fresh ginger

½ teaspoon fenugreek seeds

2 tablespoons ground coriander

1 teaspoon turmeric

1 teaspoon ground cumin

2 tablespoons ghee

1 cup thin coconut milk (see Glossary)

1 cup walnut pieces

2 tablespoons thick coconut milk

Duck is a rich meat. Here it is combined with coconut in an unusual and magnificent creamy sauce; spices give a touch of piquancy, and walnuts add texture and flavor. People say that duck was popular with the British in India, who tired of endless chicken! Any duck may be used, domestic or wild (though the flavor of the latter will be more intense). The sauce is rich, so choose at least one light vegetable, such as green peas with lovage seeds (p. 44), or fried long beans (p. 47), simple rice (p. 14) and tayar pachadi (p. 115).

1. Cut the duck into pieces around an inch square (remove the skin, if preferred). Prick the duck pieces with a fork, cover evenly with 1–2 teaspoons of salt (to taste) and let stand for an hour.

2. Peel the onions. Cut in half lengthwise and slice finely into half-rounds.

3. Deseed the fresh red chilies. Peel the garlic and ginger.

4. Finely chop the chilies, garlic and fresh ginger, add the fenugreek seeds, and grind with a mortar and pestle (or use a food processor that has a bowl for small quantities). Mix in the ground coriander, turmeric and ground cumin.

5. Heat the ghee in a heavy-based saucepan over a low heat. Brown the duck pieces. Remove and set them aside.

6. In the same ghee fry the sliced onions and brown them. Next add the ground ingredients and cook until the aroma is released. Add the thin coconut milk, cover the pan, and cook for 15 minutes.

7. Stir in the walnut pieces and the thick coconut milk, cover once more and cook for a further 5–10 minutes, or until the duck is done.

Pondicherry lamb

PANCHANAGA SEEKARANE

MAKES 8 ROULADES

3 medium onions

2 cloves garlic

1 inch fresh ginger

2 green chilies

10 blanched almonds

sprig of cilantro

1 tablespoon raisins

8 lamb leg slices, each
¼ inch thick

toothpicks or cotton thread

1 ripe mango (optional)

1 teaspoon white poppy seeds
(see Glossary)

ghee

½ teaspoon turmeric

1 teaspoon chili powder

2 teaspoons ground coriander

2 teaspoons ground cumin

½ teaspoon salt (or to taste)

1½ tablespoons plain yogurt

My French lecturer in college taught me this spiced lamb roulade dish. She was from Pondicherry, where the cooking has French influences (Tamilians in Pondicherry use a lot of fresh milk and yogurt in their cooking). So anyone who likes his sauces creamy will enjoy this recipe. Sliced fresh mangoes are added for extra flavor.

Preparation will be much easier if you ask your butcher to slice the meat for you – the slices should be no thicker than ¼ inch. Pondicherry lamb can be served with fried new potatoes (p. 59), sautéed potatoes, or saffron rice (p. 17) and a vegetable such as snow peas with ginger and chili (p. 43).

1. Peel the onions, garlic and ginger.

2. Finely chop 1 onion and half the ginger, place in a bowl. Deseed and slice the green chilies. Chop the blanched almonds. Roughly chop the cilantro.

3. Mix together all the chopped ingredients, and add the raisins. Put to one side. (MIXTURE 1.)

4. Quarter the remaining 2 onions. Place them in a food processor with the garlic and remaining ginger. Process to a pulp, or chop finely and crush with a mortar and pestle. (MIXTURE 2.)

5. Spread out the first leg slice on a plate or board. Place a heaped teaspoon of Mixture 1 in the middle and spread out a little (but not to the edges). Roll the meat lightly and secure toothpicks or cotton thread. Make all the roulades in this way.

6. If adding mango, peel and slice it thinly.

7. Grind the poppy seeds in a coffee grinder or mortar and pestle.

8. In a heavy saucepan (which will be large enough to hold the rolls of meat in one layer) heat 1 tablespoon of ghee and stir-fry Mixture 2 until golden brown. If the mixture starts to stick to the pan, a little hot water can be added.

9. Add the turmeric, chili powder, ground coriander, ground cumin, ground poppy seeds and salt.

10. Lightly beat the yogurt until smooth and add to the fried mixture in the saucepan.

11. Add the mango, if using. Stirring frequently, fry the sauce over low heat until the yogurt is blended in and takes on a yellow color.

12. Place the roulades in the mixture, turning so that they are well covered. Add a little warm water to cover, if required. Cover the pan. Lower heat and simmer gently until meat is tender (20 minutes). Adjust the sauce by adding water or mango juice if required.

Tambaram's lamb

TAMBARAM CHAKKALIKA

1 small onion

1 clove garlic

½ inch fresh ginger

3 fresh red chilies

½ teaspoon turmeric

½ teaspoon ground cumin

2 teaspoons vinegar

½ teaspoon salt (or to taste)

½ pound lamb (neck fillet)

ghee

This dish is a popular choice with young Tamilians, who love to set up makeshift beach barbecues. It is usually made with kid meat, which is available nearly all year round, but here a good alternative is tender lamb, marinated in yogurt and spices. Cook it over a barbecue or under a hot broiler.

◆ Marinate overnight for best results.

1. Peel and quarter the onion, peel the garlic and ginger. Deseed the chilies. Place them all in a food processor and reduce to a fine pulp (or chop finely and grind with a mortar and pestle). Add the turmeric, ground cumin, vinegar and salt.

2. Cut the meat into 1-inch cubes, and cover well with the paste. Leave overnight or for 8 hours.

3. Thread the cubes of meat onto skewers, and cook over a barbecue or under a hot broiler. Turn the skewers frequently and baste with melted ghee. (They will require 3–4 minutes on a hot barbecue, 5–6 under a broiler.)

Chops with peppercorns

TRICHINNAPOLLI THALLITAKARI

1 medium onion

½ inch fresh ginger

1 clove garlic

2 small fresh green chilies

sprig of cilantro

1 teaspoon cumin seeds

1 teaspoon black peppercorns

2 tablespoons raw unsalted cashew nuts

oil

1 pound lamb leg slices or loin lamb chops, or T-bone sirloin steak

1 teaspoon turmeric

1 teaspoon salt (or to taste)

3 tablespoons thick coconut milk (see Glossary) or fresh orange juice

ghee

Though this recipe, a very old one passed down to me, is called "chops," the meat is in fact cubed before cooking (your butcher can do this for you). It is best to use meat from next to the bone, however, as it is sweet and gives extra flavor to a dish. The sauce can be made with coconut milk or with fresh orange juice to brighten the flavor.

1. Peel the onion, cut in half lengthwise, and slice into thin half-rings. Peel, finely chop and crush the ginger and garlic. Deseed and finely slice the fresh green chilies. Wash and chop the cilantro.

2. Grind the cumin seeds and peppercorns in a coffee grinder or mortar and pestle.

3. Fry the cashew nuts in 1 tablespoon of oil over low heat until they are golden brown. Put to one side.

4. Cut the meat into ½-inch cubes.

5. Place the meat in a heavy-based saucepan. Add the turmeric, salt, and coconut milk (or orange juice). Heat, then simmer for 5 minutes. Set aside.

6. In a saucepan, heat 1 tablespoon of ghee and fry the thinly sliced onion until soft and golden brown. Then add the meat and fry until an aroma arises. Next add the crushed garlic, ginger and green chili. Cover the pan and cook over low heat for 10–15 minutes (there should be just a little sauce left).

7. Add the ground cumin and peppercorns, the cilantro, and the roasted cashew nuts. Mix and cook for an additional 5 minutes, then serve.

Grandma's lamb

NANDANAM BHARJITA, OR DING-DING

1 pound lean lamb

1 teaspoon salt

1 teaspoon chili powder

½ teaspoon turmeric

1 teaspoon sugar

oil

My grandmother taught me this recipe: I serve it with drinks, as an appetizer. This is an old recipe, and would have been offered to passing travelers by herdsmen, showing their hospitality. It may have been made with salt meat in the past, when salt was used as a preservative (the meat was salted and then hung outside for a day to dry), but our recipe calls for the lamb to be salted overnight. Cooking is by the fast apakava *method – deep frying.*

1. Wash the meat, slice very thinly (⅛-inch thickness) and cut into pieces about ¾ x 1½ inches. Dry thoroughly with paper towel. Sprinkle evenly with the salt and leave to marinate overnight.

2. Blot any moisture with paper towel, then place in a large bowl, sprinkle with the chili powder, turmeric and sugar, and mix well so the meat is evenly coated.

3. Deep fry the lamb strips in hot oil until crispy and dry (2–3 minutes). Drain well on paper towel.

4. Serve immediately, or allow to cool and store for up to a week in an airtight jar or container until ready to be used.

There are different terms used to address the male and female members of a Tamil family. The younger sister is called tangochi *and the older* akka, chita *is for a younger aunt and* athai *for an aunt on the father's side. Whereas* periama *means older aunt on the mother's side,* patti *is Tamil for grandmother and* puth *for great-grandmother, whereas great-aunts are called* chith-patti *or* athai-patti.

Spiced lamb

TEYNEMPET PRIYALA

1 pound lean lamb
(leg or neck fillet)

1 medium onion

2 cloves garlic

¼ inch fresh ginger

1 medium tomato

salt

1 teaspoon chili powder

1 teaspoon tomato paste

ghee or oil

¼ inch cinnamon stick

3 cardamom pods

2 whole cloves

2 teaspoons ground coriander

1 teaspoon ground cumin

This is a popular and beautifully spiced Tamilian dish, very quick to make. In the past, lamb was a royal dish, and the meat would often be cut into the shape of the Tamil gooseberry, amblikai.

I was introduced to this recipe by my six aunts, who looked after me while I was in college. I like to think that the six spices used in it represent them!

Simple rice (p. 14), or tamarind rice (p. 16), are good accompaniments.

1. Cube the meat and set aside.

2. Peel the onion and slice finely. Peel and finely chop the garlic and ginger. Roughly chop the tomato.

3. Place the meat in a saucepan with 1½ tablespoons of water, chili powder, salt to taste, tomato and the tomato paste. Cover, then simmer over medium heat for 5 minutes. Remove and set aside.

4. In another saucepan heat 1 tablespoon of ghee or oil and fry the cinnamon, cardamom and cloves until there is an aroma. Next add the sliced onions, garlic and ginger, and cook until soft. Finally add the lamb and 2 tablespoons of water, with the ground coriander and cumin. Cover and cook for an additional 10 minutes, then serve.

FACING PAGE: *Spiced lamb with tamarind rice (p. 16), fried long beans (p. 47) and just okra (p. 46)*

Lamb frikadels

NIKKAMA VESAVARA

1 pound lean ground lamb

¼ teaspoon turmeric

1 teaspoon chili powder

½ teaspoon salt (or to taste)

1 teaspoon tomato paste

1 medium onion

1 green chili

1 clove garlic

¼ inch fresh ginger

1 teaspoon cumin seeds

1 teaspoon black peppercorns

1 egg

1 cup dried breadcrumbs

oil for deep frying

These spiced meatballs became a favorite with the Dutch, who came to Madras as spice traders, and now they usually go by the Dutch name. They are a variation on an older recipe, vesavara, *which had slightly different spices. These are delicious with drinks before a meal, or as part of the main meal itself – with masala potato (see p. 56) and perhaps Nilgiris salad (p. 63).*

1. Place the ground lamb in a pan with the turmeric, chili powder, salt, tomato paste and 2 teaspoons of water. Cook gently for 5–10 minutes.

2. Peel the onion and chop finely. Deseed the green chili and slice thinly. Peel and finely chop the garlic and ginger.

3. Grind the cumin seeds and black peppercorns using a coffee grinder or crush with a mortar and pestle.

4. Fry the onion in a little oil until soft. Add the garlic, ginger, green chili and the ground spices and fry for 2–3 minutes.

5. Place the cooked ground meat, plus the fried onion mixture in a food processor and process so that the mixture becomes more even in consistency (but not as smooth as a purée). Alternatively, put through a fine grinder.

6. Separate the egg. Loosely beat the yolk and add to the mixture to bind it. Loosely beat the white and set aside.

7. Form the lamb mixture into walnut-sized balls. Dip each ball in beaten egg white and roll in the breadcrumbs.

8. Heat the oil (it should be hot enough to brown a small cube of bread instantly). Deep fry the frikadels, a few at a time, for 5 minutes. Drain on paper towel and serve warm or cold.

Masala beef

NAMBAR PADDITARAM

1 pound lean beef

salt to taste

1 teaspoon freshly ground black pepper

¼ cup cashew nuts

5–6 shallots

2 cloves garlic

1 inch fresh ginger

2 whole cloves

½ inch cinnamon stick

2 cardamom pods

½ teaspoon turmeric

1 teaspoon chili powder

1 teaspoon ground cumin

1 tablespoon ground coriander

2 teaspoons white vinegar

¼ cup hot water

½ tablespoon tamarind

ghee

cilantro

This dish was prepared for me by a college friend. The meat is cooked with tamarind – noteworthy because this combination is mentioned in early Tamil literature. The dish blends tamarind with both fiery and warm spices, and is garnished with milky-flavored cashew nuts.

1. Cut the beef into 1-inch cubes. Season with salt and black pepper. Set aside for an hour.

2. Meanwhile heat 2 teaspoons of ghee in a saucepan and fry the cashew nuts until they are golden and crisp.

3. Peel the shallots and slice finely. Peel and finely chop the garlic and ginger.

4. In a coffee grinder, or mortar and pestle, grind the cloves, cinnamon stick and cardamom pods. Place in a small bowl with the turmeric, chili powder, ground cumin and ground coriander. Add the vinegar and mix well to form a paste. Set aside.

5. Add the hot water to the tamarind. Stir with a spoon and let it infuse for 5 minutes, then strain and reserve the liquid.

6. Heat ¼ cup of ghee in a heavy-based saucepan over a medium flame, and brown the beef evenly. Remove and set aside.

7. In the same saucepan fry the garlic until brown. Then add the sliced shallots and fry until soft and golden. Next add the chopped ginger and the spice paste. Keep frying until the aroma arises. Return the browned beef to the saucepan. Lower the heat.

8. Add the tamarind liquid. Cover the pan and simmer for 15 minutes.

9. Garnish the beef with the cashew nuts and cilantro.

Beef vindaloo

VELLAKARAN VINTHELEUX

2 medium onions

2 cloves garlic

½ inch fresh ginger

4 fresh green chilies
(to taste)

3 cardamom pods

3 dried red chilies (to taste)

3 whole cloves

½ inch cinnamon stick

1 teaspoon black peppercorns

1 teaspoon fenugreek seeds

1 teaspoon cumin seeds

½ tablespoon tamarind

1 pound stew beef

ghee

piece of asafetida (size of a black
peppercorn)

¼ teaspoon salt (or to taste)

½ teaspoon turmeric

1 tablespoon ground coriander

1 tomato

1 teaspoon sugar

The lucrative spice trade between India and the West was established at least 200 years BC. Centuries later, chilies were brought from South America by the Portuguese and quickly took an important place in Tamilian cooking. From these spices Tamilians created a well-known masterpiece, said to be the hottest dish in the world.

Vindaloo is a sauce believed to purify, to heal and to cool, in accordance with Hindu philosophy. It has a unique blend of pungent red peppers, hot black ground pepper and a mixture of other spices. The recipe given is extremely hot, and most people will find this too fiery – it is best to cook it with smaller quantities of chili (the dried red chilies can be omitted completely) the first time you try it.

A dish of cooling yogurt or pachadi should be on the table when vindaloo is served. Vindaloo should be treated with respect, like the Indian tiger!

1. Peel the onions and quarter them. Chop the onions to a pulp in a food processor, or chop finely and crush with a mortar and pestle.

2. Peel the garlic and ginger, chop finely and grind to a paste. Deseed and grind the green chilies. Set aside separately.

3. Remove the seeds from the cardamom pods, discarding the pods. Deseed the dried red chilies (if using) and grind finely in a coffee grinder before adding the cardamom seeds, cloves, cinnamon stick, black peppercorns, fenugreek seeds and cumin seeds. Set aside.

4. Infuse the tamarind in ¼ cup of hot water for 8 minutes. Strain and reserve the liquid.

5. Cut the beef into 1-inch cubes.

6. Heat 2 tablespoons of ghee in a pan and fry the asafetida for a minute. Then add the cubed beef with the salt and turmeric. When browned, remove and set aside.

7. Fry the onions until soft then add the ground ginger and garlic. Return the browned meat to the pan and stir-fry for 5 minutes.

8. Add the ground green chilies, the freshly ground dried spices, and the ground coriander.

9. Roughly chop the tomato and add to the pan. Add the sugar, tamarind juice and ½ cup of hot water.

10. Cover and simmer over low heat until the meat is cooked (15–20 minutes).

Beef with chilies

TAMBRAPARNE ARACHI KOOTU

1 tablespoon tamarind

2 medium onions

1 clove garlic

4 small red fresh chilies

¼ inch fresh ginger

½ teaspoon turmeric

1 teaspoon ground cumin

2 teaspoons ground coriander

1 pound beef

oil

¼ teaspoon salt (or to taste)

1 teaspoon brown sugar

All shopping is done in small quantities in Madras, on a daily basis. Women peddling fresh produce carry on their heads baskets of fresh red chilies (maligai), sometimes with other fresh vegetables. Tamilians choose small red chilies for this fiery dish – they are often the hottest. Adjust the quantity of chili to taste, or use milder, green chilies.

1. Infuse the tamarind in ¼ cup of hot water for 8 minutes, then strain and reserve the liquid.

2. Peel the onions and slice finely. Peel and finely chop the garlic.

3. Deseed and very finely slice the fresh red chilies. Peel and finely chop or grate the ginger. Grind the chilies and ginger together in a mortar and pestle. Mix them with the turmeric, ground cumin and coriander.

4. Cut the beef into ½-inch cubes.

5. Heat 1 tablespoon of oil in a heavy-based saucepan and fry the garlic until it turns brown. Add the onion and cook until golden brown. Then add the spice mixture and fry until the aroma is released. Add the meat and stir until well covered with the spices.

6. Finally add the strained tamarind juice, sugar and salt to taste. Cover the pan and cook for an additional 10–15 minutes.

Spiced pork with orange

SUNTHAKA BHAGAYAR

1 orange

4 shallots

3 fresh red chilies

1 inch fresh ginger

1 pound lean pork fillet

ghee

½ inch cinnamon stick

½ teaspoon turmeric

1 tablespoon ground coriander

2 stalks neem leaves

2 teaspoons honey

1 teaspoon ground nutmeg

½ teaspoon salt (or to taste)

1 teaspoon freshly ground black pepper

This is a dish from the forests of Madras – home to the wild pigs, whose sweet meat reflects their foraged diet of roots and leaves (though the sweetest meat of all is that of wild pigs from the sugar plantations). It was also the forest-dwellers of times past who collected maksika, *wild honey, which they used for barter. Here the tanginess in the dish comes from freshly squeezed orange juice.*

1. Wash the orange well, then grate the zest from half of it and set aside. Squeeze the whole orange and reserve the juice. Peel and slice the shallots. De-seed and slice the fresh red chilies. Peel and finely chop the ginger. Wash and cut the pork into 1-inch cubes. Set aside

2. Grind the chilies and ginger together in a mortar and pestle.

3. Heat 1 tablespoon of ghee in a heavy-based saucepan, add the pork and cinnamon stick. Brown the pork evenly, then remove and set aside. In the same pan, fry the sliced shallots until soft and golden brown.

4. Add the ground chili and ginger, the turmeric and ground coriander, and fry for a minute, until the aroma is released. Then add the neem leaves and return the pork to the saucepan.

5. Stir in the honey, ground nutmeg, grated orange rind and 1 teaspoon of water. Add salt to taste, the black pepper, then add ¼ cup of orange juice. Cover the pan and simmer for 15–20 minutes before serving.

Pork with shallots and onion

VILLAVAR KUY

1 large onion

6 shallots

2 cloves garlic

1 inch fresh ginger

1 pound lean pork

salt to taste

2 cardamom pods

ghee

1 teaspoon chili powder

2 teaspoons ground coriander

¼ cup plain yogurt

1 teaspoon freshly ground black pepper

Wild boar has never been a forbidden meat to Hindus, and it has been carried home by hunters, villavar, *since earliest times. Hunting wild boar became a popular sport with the British in India, too.*

The use of both shallots and onion gives this recipe extra flavor, and pork will taste just as good as wild boar, if milder.

1. Peel the onion, and slice finely. Peel the shallots and slice finely. Put to one side, keeping them separate.

2. Peel and chop the garlic and ginger. Grind them together in a mortar and pestle.

3. Cut the pork into 1-inch cubes, sprinkle with a little salt and set aside.

4. In a heavy-based saucepan heat 1 tablespoon of ghee and fry the cardamom pods until the aroma is released, then add the sliced onion and cook until soft. Remove and set aside. Now fry the cubed pork until it has browned well. Remove and set aside.

5. With the saucepan off the heat, stir in the chili powder. Once the ghee turns red, place it back on the heat, add the shallots, ground ginger and garlic and fry until they are brown.

6. Add the browned pork with the ground coriander, yogurt, black pepper and 2 tablespoons of warm water. Stir well to blend, cover the pan and simmer for 10 minutes. Add the fried onions, cover the pan and cook for an additional 10 minutes, then serve.

Pork with mushrooms

CHINNE PORIKARI

6 ounces belly pork

10 ounces lean pork fillet

1 teaspoon chili powder

2 teaspoons tomato paste

1 medium onion

1 clove garlic

¼ inch fresh ginger

4 small mushrooms

oil

2 teaspoons ground coriander

¼ cup water

1 teaspoon salt (or to taste)

South India had connections with China from the earliest times, with merchants trading their wares across land and sea. Madras has always had a small Chinese community, and this recipe has a distinctive Chinese flavor with Tamilian overtones. It came to me from my grandmother, whose cook was given it by a Chinese missionary many years ago. We give dishes with a Chinese influence the name chinne *– which also means sweet. Serve with simple rice (p. 14), and vegetables such as carrots with aniseed (p. 60) and green beans.*

1. Slice the belly pork and pork fillet into small pieces. Coat them with the chili powder and tomato paste, and marinate for half an hour.

2. Peel and chop the onion coarsely. Peel the garlic and ginger, chop and crush them. Wash or wipe the mushrooms, halve them and set aside.

3. Heat 1 tablespoon of oil and fry the onion until soft. Add the pork and cook until the meat browns. Then add the ginger, garlic, ground coriander and salt to taste. Lower the heat and add the water. Cover and cook for 10 minutes.

4. Add the mushrooms, then cook for an additional 10 minutes.

Cutlets

THANJAVUR TUVAI

MAKES 8–10

3 medium potatoes

1 medium onion

1 clove of garlic

½ inch fresh ginger

1 green chili (optional)

ghee

cilantro

1 pound ground beef, lamb, pork or chicken

pinch of salt

½ teaspoon turmeric

1 teaspoon chili powder

lemon juice

1 egg

10–12 cream crackers, crushed [in U.S. substitute any plain, unsalted cracker]

oil

Tamilians refer to spicy meat made into croquettes or stuffed between mashed potatoes as cutlets, though the older name for meat ground with spices is tuvai. *This recipe was passed on to my mother from my grandmother, who was given this recipe by her mother. In Madras I use ground lamb, but in England I use ground beef, and my sisters have tried it with ground chicken. You might like to experiment, and decide which is your favorite. All three are equally delicious with a dish of green peas with lovage seeds (see p. 44).*

1. Peel the potatoes and boil until soft. Mash and put to one side.

2. Peel the onions, garlic and ginger. Chop finely. Deseed the green chili and chop finely. Finely chop the cilantro.

3. Season the meat with the salt, turmeric and chili powder.

4. Heat 1 tablespoon of ghee in a saucepan over medium heat and fry the finely chopped onion, garlic and ginger until the onion is soft and golden brown.

5. Add the ground meat, lower the heat and fry the meat in its own juices until cooked (5–8 minutes). Add the lemon juice and the chopped cilantro. Stir well, remove from the heat and allow to cool slightly.

6. Lightly beat the egg.

7. To make the cutlets, place a tablespoon of mashed potato in the palm of your hand and press firmly with the back of a spoon. Place 2 teaspoonfuls of the meat mixture in the middle. Cover with a second tablespoon of mashed potato. Press firmly between both hands to make a small potato cake. Coat with beaten egg, then dip in the cracker crumbs. Make the other cutlets in this way until the ingredients are used up.

8. Heat 3 tablespoons of oil in a wok or frying pan. Shallow fry the cutlets a few at a time, until they are golden brown, turning once. Drain on paper towel. Serve hot, with a green vegetable or salad.

Meatballs
in spicy sauce

VIRANDALI URANDAKARI KOLOMBA

1 pound ground chicken, lamb, beef or pork

¾ teaspoon turmeric

1½ teaspoons chili powder

2 teaspoons salt

2 medium onions

3 cloves garlic

1 green chili

½ inch fresh ginger

1 egg

1 tablespoon ground coriander

2 teaspoons ground cumin

2 teaspoons tomato paste

1 medium tomato

¼ inch cinnamon stick

2 whole cloves

2 cardamom pods

cilantro

1 medium potato

2 medium carrots

1½ tablespoons tamarind

ghee

Spiced meatballs of this type were popular with the British in India, and are served all over India (the Hindi name is kofta, *and the Tamil name* urandakari). *The recipe varies from region to region. These are quite small, and are cooked and served in a slightly sweet tamarind sauce, with pieces of potato (carrot can be used in place of some of the potato).*

◆ The ground meat should be marinated for as long as convenient (an hour or overnight).

1. Season the ground meat with ¼ teaspoon of the turmeric, ½ teaspoon of the chili powder, and 1 teaspoon of the salt. Leave to one side to marinate.

2. Peel and chop finely one of the onions, 1 clove garlic and half the ginger. Deseed and finely slice the green chili. Add these to the marinated meat. Separate the egg and add the yolk to the meat (reserve the white).

3. Form the meat mixture into 1-ounce balls, and set aside.

4. Peel or scrape the potatoes and carrots, and cut into ¼-inch cubes. Cover with water and set aside.

5. Infuse the tamarind in 1½ cups of hot water for 5 minutes. Strain and set the tamarind liquid to one side.

6. Make a paste with the remaining turmeric, chili powder, ground coriander, tomato paste, and a tablespoon of tamarind liquid.

7. Peel the second onion and chop coarsely. Peel and finely chop the remaining ginger and garlic. Roughly chop the tomato.

8. Beat the egg white and put to one side.

9. In a large, heavy saucepan, heat 1 tablespoon of ghee and then fry the cinnamon stick, whole cloves and cardamom pods. When the aroma is released add the spice paste, and fry until the aroma of these spices is released. Add the chopped onion, ginger and garlic, and cook until the onion softens. Then add the remaining tamarind liquid and the chopped tomato. Add the ground cumin and salt.

10. Bring the sauce to the boil and add the potato (and carrot, if using). Cover and cook gently for 10 minutes.

11. Meanwhile, carefully dip each meat ball into egg white, then lower into the boiling sauce. Cover and cook over low heat for another 10 minutes. Stir in the chopped cilantro, then cook for 5 more minutes. Serve.

Fried lambs' kidneys

POONAMALEE APAKAVA

½ pound lambs' kidneys
(or ¼ pound each kidneys and
sweetbreads)

1 medium onion

1 green chili

1 clove garlic

½ inch fresh ginger

1 teaspoon chili powder

¼ teaspoon turmeric

2 teaspoons ground coriander

1 teaspoon freshly ground black
pepper

juice of a lime

1 teaspoon salt

ghee

This dish is sometimes served with chappatis or pooris on a big circular thal, *or tray (women use a smaller one, known as a* thali*). The garlic, ginger and spices make this recipe a hot one, and the touch of lime juice tempts the appetite. It may be served as one of several dishes, or simply with chappatis as a light meal.*

1. Wash the kidneys well and cut each into quarters.

2. Peel the onion and chop coarsely. Deseed and finely slice the green chili. Peel, then chop or grate the garlic and ginger.

3. Mix the chili powder, turmeric, ground coriander and black pepper with 2 tablespoons of lime juice to form a paste. Coat the kidneys with the paste and the onion mixture. Sprinkle with the salt. Set aside to marinate for ½–1 hour.

4. Heat 2 teaspoons of ghee over low heat. Fry the onion until soft. Add the garlic, ginger and green chili, fry for a minute. Add the marinated kidneys and fry for a further 8–10 minutes (the kidneys will still be just soft). Add another 1 teaspoon of lime juice, then cook gently (covered) for 5 more minutes. Serve.

Fried chicken livers

KARUGA CHATNA

8–10 chicken livers (½ pound)

salt to taste

½ teaspoon ground turmeric

1 teaspoon chili powder

1 small onion

¼ inch fresh ginger

sprig cilantro

oil

2 teaspoons ground coriander

1 teaspoon sugar

1 teaspoon tomato paste

Cooked with a little spice, chicken livers make a delicious and tender dish, excellent as a light lunch with rice and pachadi (see p. 115). Tamilians believe that livers, because of the iron they contain, are great givers of strength – a dish to help one cope with the pressures of the world!

1. Wash the livers and cut into bite-sized pieces. Place in a dish and season with salt, the turmeric and chili powder.

2. Peel and chop the onion. Finely chop the ginger. Roughly chop the cilantro.

3. Heat 2 teaspoons of oil and fry the onions until soft, then add the ginger and fry for another minute.

4. Reduce the heat. Add the chicken livers and fry for 1 minute; add the ground coriander, sugar and tomato paste.

5. Cover and cook over low heat for 5 minutes (if the chicken liver sticks to the pan add a few spoonfuls of water and stir). Add the cilantro, cook for 2 more minutes, then serve.

According to a very old custom in Madras, a couple are remarried when the man reaches 60 years of age. Their married years are thought of as years of courtship. The wedding arrangements are carried out by the couple's children, and though it is not as elaborate and lengthy a celebration as a first wedding, it is a colorful and happy occasion. The bride wears her old golden or silver wedding sari and the man dresses in a white silk jeba *and* vesti. *Music is played on the drum before the ceremony. The husband puts another gold marriage chain or yellow string around his wife's neck, and marks her forehead with red powder. This practice was more common when girls married at the age of thirteen and men of twenty, but the marriage age has changed and these occasions are rare these days.*

Spicy calves' liver

TRIVANDRUM SHUTTURAICHI

½ pound fresh calves' liver

¼ teaspoon turmeric

1 teaspoon chili powder

¼ teaspoon salt (or to taste)

1 small onion

½ inch fresh ginger

1 small tomato

ghee

1 teaspoon tomato paste

People need strength to defend the land or work it – and liver is thought of as strengthening. Calves' liver is generally sweeter than that of the lamb or goat (often eaten in Madras). The spices contrast with it in this sizzling dish.

1. Wash and dry the liver, cut into bite-sized pieces. Cover evenly with the turmeric, chili powder and salt. Leave to marinate for half an hour.

2. Peel the onion and slice into thin rings. Peel the ginger and crush (with the side of a broad knife-blade) so the flavor will be released during cooking (it should remain a single piece). Coarsely chop the tomato.

3. Heat 2 teaspoons of ghee in a saucepan and fry the sliced onion until soft and brown. Then add the marinated liver with the crushed ginger, the tomato and tomato paste. Fry covered for 5–10 minutes, until the liver is cooked.

Spicy lambs' liver

VATHYAR PORICHAR ERAL

½ pound lambs' liver

½ teaspoon turmeric

1 teaspoon chili powder

¼ teaspoon salt (or to taste)

oil for frying

In times gone by, the arrival of someone would be celebrated by the slaughter of a goat or lamb for a feast. The liver was always considered a special delicacy. Lambs' liver is delicious when seasoned with chili powder, turmeric and salt, then simply fried.

1. Thinly slice the lambs' liver. Cover evenly with the turmeric, chili powder and salt. Leave to marinate for half an hour.

2. Fry the marinated liver in a little oil for 4–5 minutes, and serve.

CHUTNEYS, PICKLES, RELISHES

Traditionally, a Tamil meal will consist of a number of vegetable dishes, plus a chutney, with rice and yogurt. The word *chatani*, or chutney, denotes a tangy mashed or puréed vegetable dish, eaten (warm or cold) towards the end of a meal to enliven the palate. Chutneys swiftly became popular in the West, but while Western-style chutneys are generally preserves, Indian vegetable chutneys are freshly prepared each day, often from tomatoes or eggplant.

Coconut and mint are both used for a different type of chutney, which goes by the name *thambuli* or *toyal*. Coconut chutney is a traditional accompaniment to dosais (see p. 34), and mint chutney always goes with biryani (see p. 20).

Yogurt-based accompaniments, *pachadis,* are easily prepared and make a cooling, refreshing contrast to fiery or rich dishes.

Other recipes in this chapter are for sauces and pickles that accompany rice, pancakes or snacks – the most frequently prepared of all these is *sambar,* a delicious sauce for dosais (see chapter on Breads and Pancakes), rice or other snacks.

A recipe for lime pickle is also included here, of course.

Yogurt relish

TAYAR PACHADI

1 small onion

2 firm tomatoes

¼ cucumber

1 green chili

1 tablespoon plain yogurt

½ teaspoon salt

1 teaspoon sugar

cilantro

Tayar pachadi is a frequent choice of dish at weddings, where it is served alongside biryani, for its simplicity contrasts with the richness of biryani and other rich food. The yogurt in pachadi is also cooling, and good with fiery dishes. This onion and tomato pachadi is very quick and easy to prepare, and a Tamil housewife (who will generally cook two or three vegetable dishes) will often make pachadi if she finds herself running out of time. (In north India, pachadi goes by the name of raita.)

1. Peel and chop the onion. Cut the tomatoes and cucumber into small cubes.

2. Deseed the green chili and slice thinly. Add to the chopped vegetables.

3. Gently mix in the yogurt, then the salt and sugar. Leave to stand for a short while for the flavors to develop.

4. Serve garnished with cilantro.

Most Tamilians speak at least three languages: Tamil, English (which for many years was the official language), and Hindi (the present official language). Tamilians living in Pondicherry speak French as well. People who live near the Andhra border speak Urdu or Telugu, while Tamilians living in Ootacamund speak Malayalam and the local dialect of Verdoid origin. Some Tamil words have been absorbed into the English language – "chutney" and "curry" are two examples.

Coconut chutney

TEYNGA THOYAL

½ teaspoon tamarind

half a fresh coconut

3 fresh green chilies

1 teaspoon split chickpeas (channa dhall)

1 teaspoon salt

peanut oil

1 teaspoon mustard seeds

1 teaspoon roasted split chickpeas (channa dhall)

½ teaspoon cleaned split black grams (urad dhall)

4–5 neem leaves

¼ teaspoon sugar

Coconut chutney is always served with dosais and idlis. The chilies add a touch of fire to the sweetness of the coconut.

1. Infuse the tamarind in 2 teaspoons of hot water for 3 minutes. Strain the liquid and set aside.

2. Finely grate the white pulp of the coconut (in a food processor, if available).

3. Deseed and finely chop the green chilies. Thoroughly wash the unroasted channa dhall. Add both, plus the salt, to the coconut in the food processor, and process until quite smooth.

4. Heat 1 tablespoon of oil in a saucepan. Fry the mustard seeds, roasted channa dhall, urad dhall and neem leaves. When the mustard seeds pop and the dhall is golden brown, add the ingredients to the ground coconut and tamarind liquid. Add the sugar and serve.

Mint chutney

POODINA

½ teaspoon tamarind

3 green chilies

¼ pound fresh mint leaves

salt to taste

1 teaspoon sugar

Cilantro and mint are important ingredients in Tamilian cooking, and add a sweetish, refreshing flavor to a meal. In this recipe the addition of tamarind and chilies gives the chutney a little extra bite. It is generally served with biryani, and with various types of pancakes. The tamarind acts as a preservative, and poodina *can be stored for about a week in the refrigerator.*

1. Infuse the tamarind in ¼ cup of hot water for 5 minutes. Strain the liquid and set aside.

2. Deseed and roughly chop the green chilies.

3. Wash the mint thoroughly and chop roughly. (If the stems are very tough they can be discarded.)

4. Put all the ingredients in a food processor and process to an even consistency. Remove and keep cool.

Traditionally, a Tamil woman's main role is that of a mother, and women who do not bear children may be scorned by society – newly married Tamil women are given young coconuts by their mothers and mothers-in-law, as a symbol of fertility.

Eggplant chutney

KATRIKA CHATANI

2 eggplants

2 soft tomatoes

1 medium onion

2 fresh green chilies

2 cloves garlic

3 whole cloves

1 teaspoon cinnamon

peanut oil

salt

2 tablespoons plain yogurt (if serving cold)

sprig cilantro

Tamilians love to go picnicking on weekends or festival days. As Madras is near the coast, many families go to the seaside and they invariably invite other relatives and their families to go with them.

Chutneys are popular picnic dishes, as they can be eaten hot or cold and are ideal accompaniments to many dishes. This eggplant chutney is always made fresh and is eaten in larger quantities than Western-style chutney preserves.

1. Cut the eggplant and tomatoes into fine dice, then place in a pan with ½ cup of water, bring to the boil, and simmer for 5–10 minutes or until cooked.

2. Meanwhile peel the onion and slice finely. Deseed and slice the green chilies. Peel and crush the garlic. Grind the cloves.

3. Drain the cooked vegetables, let them cool slightly, then mash. Set aside.

4. Heat 1 tablespoon of oil and fry the onions, green chilies and garlic with the cloves and cinnamon, until soft. Add the mashed eggplant and tomatoes, season with salt to taste and cook for another 5 minutes.

5. Serve the chutney warm or allow it to cool, then add the yogurt. Garnish with cilantro.

Tomato chutney

AKKAS TAKALI CHATANEE

2–3 firm red tomatoes (or a mixture of red and yellow tomatoes)

½ tablespoon tamarind

6 shallots

2 cloves garlic

½ inch fresh ginger

2–3 fresh green chilies (to taste)

sprig cilantro

ghee or oil

asafetida, a piece the size of a black peppercorn

1 teaspoon black mustard seeds

1 teaspoon fenugreek seeds

1 teaspoon split cleaned black grams (urad dhall)

¼ teaspoon cumin seeds

¼ teaspoon turmeric

1 teaspoon salt

2 tablespoons brown sugar

This tomato chutney is delicious, both sweet and piquant. Best served at room temperature, it is a good accompaniment to almost any dish. I like to use both red and yellow tomatoes for my tomato chatanee.

1. Pour boiling water over the tomatoes and allow to stand for a minute or two. Remove their skins and chop coarsely.

2. Infuse the tamarind in ¼ cup of hot water for 5 minutes. Strain and put the liquid to one side.

3. Peel and quarter the shallots. Peel and roughly slice the garlic and ginger. Deseed the chilies.

4. Finely chop the shallots.

5. Grind together the garlic, ginger and fresh green chilies in a food processor, or chop finely and grind with a mortar and pestle.

6. Roughly chop the cilantro.

7. In a heavy-based saucepan heat 1 tablespoon of ghee (or oil) until it starts to sizzle. Add the asafetida, the black mustard seeds, fenugreek seeds, split cleaned black grams and cumin seeds and cook until they pop and turn golden brown – take care that they do not burn. Then add the shallots.

8. Stir in the ground garlic mixture and turmeric, and cook until golden brown.

9. Next add the chopped tomatoes, cilantro, tamarind juice, salt and sugar. Reduce the heat, cover the pan and cook for 5 minutes.

10. Serve at room temperature. (It will keep for up to a week in the refrigerator, stored in an airtight container.)

Mango chutney

MAMBALAM MANGAI PRALEKA

3–4 ripe mangoes (12 ounces prepared weight)

1½ cups dark brown sugar (equal to volume of prepared fruit)

½ inch fresh ginger

4 cloves garlic

4 dried dates

peanut oil

2 teaspoons fenugreek seeds

2 teaspoons mustard seeds

1 tablespoon turmeric

1 teaspoon salt

2 teaspoons chili powder

½ cup raisins

¼ cup slivered almonds

Mangoes have three special qualities that have been extolled for nearly 3000 years: they are said to be sacred (their leaves are hung over the threshold on important occasions), help fulfil wishes, and are considered the arrows of Mannatha, the Indian Cupid – so are lucky in matters of love. Mango chutneys were brought back to England by the East India Company. This simple chatani embodies the six tastes which form part of the Indian meal: sweet, sour, bitter, salty, astringent and pungent. This chutney will keep for 2–3 weeks in the refrigerator.

1. Wash and peel the mangoes. Cut into fine cubes, ⅛ inch in size. Measure the mango cubes, and measure an equal amount of brown sugar.

2. Peel and finely chop the ginger and garlic. Chop the dates.

3. Heat 2 tablespoons of oil in a heavy-based saucepan, and fry the fenugreek, mustard seeds and turmeric. Add the mango cubes, then the sugar, chili powder, garlic, ginger, raisins, dates and almonds. Stir well.

4. Cook gently, stirring occasionally, for an hour over low heat. Cool and serve or store in an airtight jar.

Eggplant with tamarind and coconut

DEVANAYAGAM PULI KOLAMBA

1 onion

2 tomatoes

3 small eggplants

1 tablespoon tamarind

ghee

1 teaspoon fenugreek seeds

2 teaspoons ground coriander

1 teaspoon chili powder

1 teaspoon salt

½ cup thick coconut milk (see Glossary)

My mother learned this dish from my father's mother, and it always reminds me of happy childhood days. This sauce is a speciality of the Nadar community, and combines coconut with eggplant and sweet–tart tamarind. This rather thin sauce is eaten poured over rice.

1. Peel and chop the onion coarsely. Cut the eggplant into ¼-inch dice, and finely slice the tomato.

2. Infuse the ball of tamarind in 6 tablespoons of hot water for about 5 minutes. Strain and put this thick liquid to one side, retaining the tamarind pulp. Infuse the same pulp in another 4 tablespoons of water for 5 minutes. Strain and put this thin liquid to one side, keeping it separate from the first batch. Discard the pulp.

3. Heat 1 teaspoon of ghee in a saucepan and fry the fenugreek seeds until the aroma is released and they turn brown. Then add the coarsely chopped onion. Fry until soft and golden brown.

4. Stir in the ground coriander, chili powder and salt. Add the first (thick) batch of tamarind liquid, and simmer for 3–5 minutes.

5. Add the prepared tomato and eggplant, and ½ cup of water. Simmer for a minute before adding the second infusion of tamarind.

6. Next add the coconut milk and cook for a minute or two.

7. Raise the heat. Add another ¼ cup of water. Bring back to the boil and finish cooking for 10–15 minutes, until the eggplant and tomatoes are soft. The sauce will have a pouring consistency.

Lime pickle

ELAMCHA URGA

MAKES 2 8-OUNCE JARS

10 limes

2 tablespoons white vinegar

1 tablespoon salt

¼ cup brown sugar

½ pound dates

4 cloves garlic

1 inch ginger

1 teaspoon cumin seeds

2 teaspoons mustard seeds

2 tablespoons chili powder

Lime pickle is a preserve, so is not made when required as the chutneys are. It has a sharp, sweet–sour flavor that improves with keeping. The flavor is strong, so the pickle should be used sparingly, a teaspoonful per person at most. Unlike many recipes, which need the limes to stand for several days, this recipe of my mother's speeds up the pickle-making process by precooking the limes.

1. Quarter the limes, removing some or all of the seeds. Place in a heavy pan or wok, with the vinegar, salt and sugar, cover the pan and simmer over very low heat until the limes have softened (around 15 minutes).

2. Grind the dates, garlic and ginger in a mortar and pestle.

3. Heat 1 tablespoon of oil and fry the cumin and mustard seeds. Remove from the heat and add the vinegar used to boil the limes.

4. Add the chili powder, return to the heat, and stir until the chili has cooked.

5. Slowly add the ground dates, ginger and garlic. Stir well.

6. Finally add the limes and boil for 2 minutes.

7. Allow to cool a little, then pour into heated, sterilized jars. Seal while warm.

The daily life of the Hindu is affected by the five elements: sky, air, water, fire and earth, and by the times of the day: dawn, morning, afternoon, evening, dusk and night. This pickle is generally made around noon. Certain spices, such as chili, are believed to produce heat in the body, and others to cool it down. Limes and all citrus fruits are considered cooling. Lime pickle, combining chili and citrus, has both these elements.

Drumstick sambar

RUNGASWAMY MURANGAKAI SAMBAR

1 drumstick (see Glossary)

⅔ cup red grams (toor dhall)

2 cloves garlic

1 teaspoon turmeric

1 teaspoon salt

1 tablespoon tamarind

1 medium-sized onion

1 tomato

ghee

1 teaspoon black mustard seeds

2 dried red chilies

1 teaspoon ground cumin

This is a recipe that reflects the season. In the month of May Tamil women dress in yellow saris and perform the folk dance called the Bhangra, to celebrate the beginning of the Hindi solar year. The sunshine is reflected in the turmeric used in this recipe. Sambar is a rich yellow-colored, slightly sweet sauce of lentils, flavored with onion, tamarind, black mustard seed and "drumsticks" – a long, stick-like vegetable containing a sweet pulp that adds its own unique flavor to the sauce. (Sambar can also be made with other vegetables, such as eggplant.) This sauce is traditionally served with rice, and with dosais.

1. Wash and cut the drumstick into 2-inch lengths. Wash the toor dhall. Peel and crush cloves of garlic

2. Place the toor dhall, turmeric and salt in a pan with 1½ cups of boiling water. Cook half-covered for 10 minutes, then add the prepared drumsticks and crushed garlic to the lentils. Cover and cook for an additional 15 minutes (the dhall should be quite soft).

3. Meanwhile infuse the tamarind in ¼ cup of hot water for 5 minutes. Strain and put the liquid to one side.

4. Peel and slice the onion finely. Chop the tomato.

5. In a saucepan heat 1 tablespoon of ghee and fry the onion until soft. Add the black mustard seeds and continue cooking until the seeds pop.

6. Add the onion mixture, the tamarind juice, dried red chilies, ground cumin and tomato to the dhall mixture, and simmer for another 15 minutes. The sambar should be a fairly thin sauce.

Pepper water

RASSAM

1 teaspoon black peppercorns

1½ teaspoons cumin seeds

2 cloves garlic

1 tablespoon tamarind

1 tomato

ghee

salt

asafetida (size of a small marble)

2 neem leaves

An important aspect of the Hindu faith is healing. Peppercorns, known to Tamil Hindus for their healing qualities, are used to make rassam, or "pepper water" as it is sometimes called. This deliciously aromatic liquid has the acid sweetness of tamarind and the fire of the peppercorns. Rassam is a very thin sauce, traditionally served spooned over rice. Rassam remaining at the end of the meal is often drunk, to cleanse the palate.

1. Grind or crush the black peppercorns, cumin seeds and cloves of garlic together in a mortar and pestle.

2. Meanwhile infuse the tamarind in ½ cup of hot water for 5–10 minutes. Strain and set the juice aside. Wash and chop the tomato.

3. In a saucepan heat 1 teaspoon of ghee. Fry the crushed black peppercorns, cumin seeds and garlic cloves with the asafetida until there is an aroma. Then pour in the tamarind juice and add salt to taste. Raise the heat and bring to the boil. Add the tomato and neem leaves. Reduce the heat and let it simmer for 2–5 minutes.

TIFFIN

SAVORY AND SWEET SNACKS, DESSERTS AND DRINKS

No day is complete without tiffin, India's afternoon snack, to fill the gap between lunch and dinner. There are mobile carts, coffee shops, sweetshops and cafés on every street in Madras, selling sweets and savories with coffee and tea. In Tamil cuisine, savory and sweet snacks are not thought of as separate and distinct, so they are sold together – consequently, this chapter contains a selection of both.

In the West there is plenty of scope for preparing these dishes outside tiffin-time. Many of the savory tiffin snacks are perfect for picnics or for party buffets, while the sweet tiffin dishes here can be served as desserts, or as sweetmeats with after-dinner coffee.

(A dessert in Madras will often be simply fresh fruit – juicy mangoes, crisp apples, sweet bananas, custard apples, oranges, jackfruits [similar to breadfruit], exotic pomegranates and papayas, sweet grapes, plums and pears, and even strawberries may combine to create a temptingly delightful, delicious and colorful display. Young coconuts sometimes make a dessert by themselves.)

SAVORIES

Savory snacks are usually made from very basic ingredients. Some, such as *bondas,* are made from cleaned split black grams (urad dhall). Others, such as *uppuma,* are made from semolina, a wheat product. *Samosas,* deep-fried triangular pastry parcels, are made from self-rising flour and stuffed with meat or vegetables. Eggs are both versatile and cheap, and this chapter begins with several simple and commonly used egg recipes.

Spicy eggs

RAJKUMARAN MASALA MUTTA

4 eggs

1 medium onion

1 clove garlic

½ inch fresh ginger

2 ripe tomatoes

oil

1 teaspoon chili powder

½ teaspoon turmeric

salt to taste

1½ teaspoons ground coriander

½ teaspoon ground cumin

1 teaspoon fenugreek seeds

1 tablespoon tamarind

Tamilians love cricket as much as the English do, and have equal enthusiasm for the cricket tea! However, the food served has its own Tamilian flavor and instead of sandwiches and hard-boiled eggs, the cricketers in Madras enjoy spicy eggs on pooris, samosas, pakoras, cutlets and sweetmeats. Spicy eggs are ideal for hot lazy days in summer (they also make a more substantial meal, served with rice and a vegetable dish).

1. Hard boil the eggs, then cool and shell them.

2. Peel and finely slice the onion. Peel and finely chop the garlic and ginger. Roughly chop the tomatoes.

3. Fry the sliced onion in a little oil until soft. Then add the garlic and ginger and cook until brown.

4. Add the chili powder, turmeric, salt, ground coriander and ground cumin, and continue frying for 5 minutes.

5. Add the fenugreek seeds and reduce the heat, then add the tomatoes. Cover and simmer until the tomatoes are soft and pulpy.

6. Meanwhile infuse the tamarind in ¼ cup of hot water for 5 minutes. Mix well and strain the liquid. Stir the tamarind liquid into the tomato mixture and add the whole hard-boiled eggs. Increase the temperature and cook the dish for a few minutes. Serve hot.

Madras omelette

CHEYNAIPATTINAM OMELETTE

1 medium onion

2 cloves garlic

1 small tomato

2 fresh green chilies

4 eggs

1 teaspoon freshly ground black pepper

salt to taste

2 tablespoons butter

sprig cilantro

The omelette is a favorite dish in both the East and the West, but omelettes in North America, Britain, France or Madras are, of course, delightfully different. Half the fun of cooking is using one's imagination and skill with the ingredients to hand. This is my grandmother's recipe, a truly Tamilian one.

1. Peel and finely chop the onion. Peel and finely chop the garlic. Roughly chop the tomato. Deseed and finely slice the fresh chilies.

2. Break the eggs into a bowl and beat well. Season with salt and black pepper. Then add all the chopped ingredients.

3. Melt the butter in an omelette pan over low heat. When the butter is hot add the mixture and cook gently until the omelette is set and it is golden brown on both sides (turn it halfway through cooking). Remove from the pan and serve hot, garnished with cilantro.

Scrambled eggs

KIRKANNA MUTTA

1 medium onion

2 cloves garlic

1 medium tomato

2 fresh green chilies

2 tablespoons butter

4 eggs

salt to taste

sprig cilantro

I like my eggs scrambled with onions, chilies, tomatoes, garlic and butter in the evening, with dosais (see p. 34). This recipe gives the otherwise bland eggs a bit of bite!

1. Peel the onion and chop finely. Peel and finely chop the garlic. Wash and finely chop the tomato (peel first if preferred). Deseed and finely slice the fresh chilies.

2. Melt the butter over low heat, and add the onion. Fry until soft. Add the garlic, chilies and tomatoes. Finally add the eggs one at a time and mix gently. Salt to taste. Cook, stirring, until scrambled. Remove and serve hot, garnished with cilantro.

Bondas

ANNA NAGAR

2 green chilies

3–4 black peppercorns

sprig cilantro

2 tablespoons plain yogurt

1 teaspoon baking soda

⅔ cup black gram (urad dhall) flour (see Glossary)

1 teaspoon cumin seeds

¼ teaspoon salt (or to taste)

oil

Bondas are balls of spiced black gram (urad dhall) batter the size of a walnut, deep fried so they are brown on the outside and creamy soft on the inside. In Madras, they are served in large leaves, and are accompanied by coconut chutney (see p. 116).

1. Deseed and finely chop the green chilies. Lightly crush the black peppercorns with a mortar and pestle. Wash and chop the cilantro.

2. Whisk the yogurt in a bowl with ½ cup of water and the baking soda until smooth, then sift in the black gram flour. Add the cumin seeds, crushed black peppercorns, green chilies, cilantro and salt. Beat well with a wooden spoon.

3. Heat oil for deep frying. Test the temperature by dropping in a small cube of bread – it should slowly rise to the top, and the oil should not smoke. Drop in 1 tablespoon of batter at a time. (Lower the heat, or the outside of the bondas will brown before they are cooked inside.) Fry the bondas until golden brown. Drain on paper towel and serve hot, with coconut chutney.

Samosas with meat filling

KARAJIGE TUVAI

MAKES 24

Ingredients for filling:

½ pound ground meat (lamb, chicken or beef)

¼ teaspoon turmeric

½ teaspoon chili powder

salt

½ medium onion

1 clove garlic

⅛ inch fresh ginger

½ fresh red chili

1 whole clove

1 cardamom pod

ghee

¼ teaspoon ground coriander

¼ teaspoon ground cumin

½ teaspoon freshly squeezed lime juice

These bring back memories of my college days, sitting beneath the eucalyptus with friends, all of us munching our samosas.

Samosas are deep-fried pastry triangles with a meat or vegetable filling. Lamb, chicken or beef can be used for the filling (usually chosen according to season – lamb in spring or autumn, chicken in summer, beef in the cooler winter).

The pastry of the samosas should be light and crisp, with extra crunch from onion seeds. If the pastry is light enough to the touch it can be folded over twice to get a crispy effect.

◆ Marinate the filling for at least an hour before use.

FILLING

1. Marinate the ground meat with the turmeric and chili powder and salt to taste for at least 1 hour.

2. Peel the onion and chop finely. Peel and finely chop the garlic, ginger and red chili.

3. Grind the cloves and cardamom pods using a coffee grinder or a mortar and pestle.

4. Heat 2 tablespoons of ghee in a pan. Fry the onion until soft and light brown. Add the garlic, ginger and chili and fry until soft.

5. Add the marinated meat and the ground coriander, cumin, cloves and cardamom pods. Cover the pan and cook for about 10 minutes (if the mixture becomes dry add 1 or 2 teaspoons of hot water).

6. Stir in the lime juice, cook for another minute, then allow to cool.

Ingredients for pastry:

Note: *To obtain the required consistency it is essential to make the dough with water and ghee that are lukewarm (felt with the finger they will seem neither hot nor cold).*

2 cups self-rising flour

2 tablespoons ghee

½ cup water

pinch of salt

1 teaspoon onion seeds

PASTRY AND ASSEMBLY

1. Mix all the ingredients and knead to a very soft, pliable dough. Cover with a damp cloth or plastic wrap and leave to rest for 10 minutes.

2. To make 24 3-inch squares of pastry, divide the pastry into 8 evenly sized balls, roll out each ball to a piece 3 inches wide and 9 inches long. Cut into 3 squares.

3. Fill the squares with the cooked meat mixture (the dough should be very stretchy and easy to handle):

- place a teaspoon of filling in the middle of a square of pastry;
- fold up the bottom right corner diagonally, to a point ¾ inch from the top edge and ¾ inch from the left edge (stretch the dough if necessary);
- moisten the L-shaped border that is formed, fold it over the triangular flap (it will be double thickness at the corner) and seal;
- twist the dough tightly at all three corners, to make a firm little spiky-cornered triangular pasty.

Make the other samosas in the same way.

4. Heat oil for deep frying (check temperature with a cube of bread: it should turn brown immediately when dropped in), or set an electric deep fryer to its hottest temperature. Deep fry the samosas a few at a time until golden brown. Drain on paper towel and serve hot.

Vegetable samosas

NANDANAM KARAJIKAYI

Vegetable samosas are generally bigger than meat-filled ones, as the vegetables are not ground but chopped finely. Vegetable samosas are ideal tiffin, since they contain both "heating" (potatoes, carrots) and "cooling" (peas, tomatoes) vegetables. Parsnip or rutabaga could be used as an alternative root vegetable.

MAKES 18

Ingredients for filling:

3 tablespoons shelled peas, fresh or frozen

1 small carrot

1 medium potato

¼ head cauliflower

2 or 3 green beans

1 medium onion

2 cloves of garlic

¼ inch fresh ginger

ghee

2 whole cloves

2 cardamom pods

½ teaspoon turmeric

1 teaspoon chili powder

¼ teaspoon ground cumin

¼ teaspoon ground coriander

salt

1 teaspoon freshly squeezed lime juice

FILLING

1. Defrost the peas (or any other frozen vegetable) if necessary.

2. Peel and parboil the carrot and the potato separately. Cut into small cubes (¼ inch).

3. Discard the cauliflower stalks, and cut or break the remainder into tiny florets. Finely chop the green beans. Peel and finely chop the onion, garlic and ginger.

4. Heat 2 tablespoons of ghee in a heavy saucepan. Add the cloves and cardamom pods.

5. Add the finely chopped onion and fry until soft and brown. Then fry the garlic and ginger with the onion.

6. Add the turmeric and chili powder. Fry for 1 minute and then add the diced carrots and potatoes; fry for another 3 minutes until they are nearly soft.

7. Stir in the ground cumin and coriander. If the mixture is dry add 1 tablespoon of water.

8. Finally add the green beans and peas, salt to taste, and cook for another 5 minutes.

9. Before the end of cooking stir in the lime juice. Allow to cool.

Ingredients for pastry:

Note: *To obtain the required consistency it is essential to make the dough with water and ghee that are lukewarm (felt with the finger they will seem neither hot nor cold).*

2 cups self-rising flour

2 tablespoons ghee

½ cup water

pinch of salt

1 teaspoon onion seeds

oil

PASTRY AND ASSEMBLY

1. Mix all the ingredients and knead to a very soft, pliable dough. Cover with a moist cloth or plastic wrap and leave to rest for 10 minutes.

2. To make 18 3½-inch squares of pastry, divide the pastry into 6 evenly sized balls, roll out each ball to a piece 3½ inches wide and 10½ inches long. Cut into 3 squares.

3. Fill the squares with the filling (the dough should be very stretchy and easy to handle):

- place a teaspoon of filling in the middle of a square of pastry;

- fold up the bottom right corner diagonally, to a point ¾ inch from the top edge and ¾ inch from the left edge (stretch the dough if necessary);

- moisten the L-shaped border that is formed, fold it over the triangular flap (it will be double thickness at the corner) and seal;

- twist the dough tightly at all three corners, to make a firm little spiky-cornered triangular pasty.

Make the other samosas in the same way.

4. Heat oil for deep frying (check temperature with a cube of bread: it should turn brown immediately when dropped in), or set an electric deep fryer to its hottest temperature. Deep fry the samosas a few at a time until golden brown. Drain on paper towel and serve hot.

Savory semolina and legume snack

ATHAI'S UPPUMA

1 medium onion

2 green chilies

sprig cilantro

½ cup coarse semolina

1 teaspoon split chickpeas (channa dhall)

1 teaspoon cleaned split black grams (urad dhall)

1 teaspoon brown mustard seeds

asafetida (piece the size of a black peppercorn)

2–3 neem leaves

1 cup boiling water

1 teaspoon fresh lime juice

salt

Uppuma has the texture of coarse breadcrumbs, and is a typical spicy Tamilian tiffin dish. My aunt used to make the most wonderful uppuma, and often served it as tiffin on Mondays when she was pressed for time.

1. Peel and finely chop the onion. Deseed the chilies and slice very finely. Chop the cilantro.

2. Heat 1 tablespoon of ghee (preferably in a nonstick pan or wok) and fry the semolina until golden brown. Remove and put aside.

3. Add the onion to the hot ghee and fry until soft but not brown.

4. Add both the grams, green chili, mustard seeds, asafetida and halved neem leaves. Fry for a minute, then gradually pour the boiling water onto the mixture, stirring constantly.

5. When the mixture comes to the boil, gradually stir in the fried semolina, then add the lime juice, salt to taste and chopped cilantro. Cook, stirring continuously, for about 5 minutes or until the semolina is cooked. The mixture should take on the consistency of coarse breadcrumbs.

Spiced lentil cakes

VADAIS

MAKES ABOUT 12

½ cup split chickpeas (channa dhall)

½ cup split black grams (urad dhall)

2 small onions

¼ inch fresh ginger

2 green chilies

1 egg yolk

oil

pinch salt

¼ teaspoon turmeric

2 or 3 neem leaves

Vadais *are lentil cakes, a delicious spicy snack sold in coffee shops with hot sweet tea, or* chaya.

The mixture is traditionally made without egg, but it makes the dough much easier to handle. Serve with coconut chutney (p. 116) or sambar (p. 122).

◆ The grams and chickpeas need to be soaked for at least 3 hours (or overnight) before cooking.

1. Soak the grams and chickpeas in water for 3 hours. Rinse and strain. Place in a food processor with 2 teaspoons of water and grind coarsely.

2. Peel the onions and chop finely. Peel and finely chop the ginger. Deseed and finely slice the green chilies. Loosely beat the egg yolk.

3. Heat 1 teaspoon of oil and fry the onion, ginger, green chili and neem leaves until soft. Add the turmeric and salt, and fry for a minute or two.

4. Add the fried ingredients to the dhall mixture, and add just enough beaten egg yolk to bind the mixture.

5. Form the mixture into walnut-sized balls; flatten them slightly.

6. Heat 1–2 inches of oil in a wok, and fry the vadais a few at a time until reddish brown on both sides. Drain on paper towel.

Pakoras

ROYAPETTA PAKORAS

Pakoras are eaten all over India, but originated in the south. In the north they are often eaten with a meal (and, confusingly, are some-times called bhajis*), whereas in Tamil Nadu they are eaten as a snack.*

These lovely battered vegetables can be prepared with eggplant, onions or potatoes. They are deep fried until crisp on the outside, and served hot or cold as an appetizing crispy snack with drinks, accompanied by coconut or mint chutney (see p. 116).

◆ The batter needs to stand for at least half an hour before use.

MAKES ABOUT 30 PAKORAS

For the batter:

2 cups gram [chickpea] flour

¼ teaspoon baking powder

½ teaspoon chili powder

¼ teaspoon turmeric

2 teaspoons ground coriander

2 teaspoons ground cumin

¼ teaspoon salt (or to taste)

2 tablespoons plain whole milk yogurt

1 cup cold water

vegetables: a small onion (about 2 ounces), potato (3 ounces) or eggplant (3 ounces) — or a mixture of the three

oil

1. Prepare the batter. Mix all the dry ingredients in a bowl. Slowly beat in the yogurt, then the water, to form a thick, smooth batter. Beat it well and allow to stand for at least half an hour.

2. Peel the vegetables and cut into slices ⅛ inch thick. If they are not to be used immediately, soak in a bowl of salted water to prevent them turning brown. Drain and pat dry before use.

3. Heat 2–3 inches of oil in a wok or deep fryer – do not allow it to smoke. Beat the batter again lightly. Dip each piece of vegetable in the batter to coat lightly, and fry until golden brown. Drain on paper towel. Serve hot or cold, with coconut or mint chutney.

FACING PAGE: *Samosas (pp. 128 and 130), vadais (p. 133) and pakoras (p. 134)*

Onion bhajis

VENGAYAM PAGODAS

MAKES ABOUT 10–12

2 large onions (10 ounces total)

¼ inch fresh ginger

3–4 green chilies

sprig cilantro

1 teaspoon salt

¼ teaspoon turmeric

½ teaspoon chili powder

¼ teaspoon ground cumin

1 cup gram [chickpea] flour

1 teaspoon peanut oil, warmed

½ cup iced water

for the sauce (optional):

¼ cup plain yogurt

a few fresh mint leaves

These are a great favorite in the Madras coffee houses. The fine onion rings are mixed into a gram-flour batter, then spoonfuls are deep fried until crisp and crunchy on the outside and a little softer inside. The secret of the batter is the careful addition of water once the dry ingredients have been mixed thoroughly with a fork or fingertips. As a variation, a few roasted peanuts can be added to the batter before frying.

1. Peel the onions and cut into ⅛-inch slices. Separate the slices into individual rings and place in a mixing bowl.

2. Peel the ginger, and chop finely. Deseed the chilies and slice finely. Wash and roughly chop the cilantro. Place all the chopped ingredients in the bowl with the onion rings.

3. Add the salt, turmeric, chili powder, cumin and gram flour. Mix well with a fork or fingertips.

4. Add the warm oil and water, and mix thoroughly – it should form a thick batter that will fall easily from a spoon. Allow to stand for half an hour.

5. Heat a few inches of oil in a wok or deep fryer. Carefully drop tablespoonfuls of batter into the hot oil and deep fry over medium heat, a few at a time, until crisp and reddish-brown. Remove from the oil and drain on paper towel. Best served while still warm, especially with a sauce of a few chopped mint leaves stirred into yogurt.

Chickpeas

VELLANKANI SUNDAL

1 cup dried chickpeas

½ teaspoon turmeric

salt to taste

oil

10 neem leaves

2 fresh green chilies

1 teaspoon black mustard seeds

asafetida (piece the size of a black peppercorn)

cilantro

2 tablespoons grated fresh coconut

This dish makes a good accompaniment to a summer meal, or as a titbit with drinks.

Chickpeas are grown near Trichinapalli, famous for its temples and the Red Fort with its mosque, with a dome said to be sculpted in gold. Here, in May each year, a Hindu festival called Pooram is held to celebrate the new moon. Elephants decked with ceremonial umbrellas bless the pilgrims with their trunks in return for a small donation to the temple. Young boys sell this tasty chickpea snack to visitors, for them to munch on their way back to the city.

1. Soak the dried chickpeas overnight in plenty of water.

2. Rinse the chickpeas and place, with the turmeric and salt to taste, into a heavy-based saucepan or a pressure cooker, and add enough water to cover them. Cook the chickpeas until tender (around an hour, or 15 minutes under pressure). Strain excess water after cooking and set aside.

3. Meanwhile wash the neem leaves and remove their stems. Deseed and slice the fresh green chilies.

4. Heat 1 teaspoon of oil in a saucepan. Fry the mustard seeds until they pop. Then add the asafetida, sliced green chilies, neem leaves and chickpeas. Stir-fry for about 5 minutes until the ingredients in the saucepan are mixed well.

5. Remove from the pan, and garnish with fresh coconut and cilantro.

Muruku

MAKES ABOUT 24

1 cup rice flour

1 cup gram [chickpea] flour

1 cup all-purpose flour

1 teaspoon cumin seeds

1 teaspoon salt

2 teaspoons chili powder

pinch of ground asafetida

2 tablespoons butter

1 teaspoon sesame seeds

oil

Muruku *are deep-fried titbits made of gram and rice flour – they are crunchy and delicious and make an excellent snack or predinner nibble with drinks.* Muruku *keep well, for a few days, in an airtight container. They are usually made with a* muruku *press, but a pastry bag works just as well.*

1. Sift together the flours, mix well and set aside.

2. In a heavy-based saucepan combine the water with cumin seeds, salt, chili powder, ground asafetida and butter and bring to the boil.

3. When it comes to the boil, remove from the heat and stir in the sesame seeds and half the sifted flours.

4. Add the rest of the flour, stirring until the mixture holds together. Gradually add just enough water to obtain a soft dough. Knead lightly for 1 minute.

5. Flour the work surface or cover with a large piece of foil. Put the soft dough into a pastry bag with a ¼-inch plain nozzle. Force out dough mixture onto the foil, to form rings or figure eights 2½ inches across.

6. Heat a few inches of oil in a wok for deep frying, over medium heat.

7. Gently slide each muruku onto a spatula and lower the muruku into the hot oil. Fry until golden brown and crisp (2–5 minutes). Drain well on paper towel. Repeat the process until the dough is used up.

8. Cool and store in an airtight container.

SWEETS AND DESSERTS

Sweetmeats are symbols of welcome, love and hospitality, and are eaten at almost any time of day. Sweets are always eaten at religious festivals, which are considered to be happy occasions, when friends and relatives share a feast of sweetmeats and also give them to the poor.

Many sweet dishes are based on milk enriched with nuts of all varieties. Indian ice cream, known as *kulfi*, is a well-known example. Nuts are important for their protein and add richness to sweet dishes. Peanuts, cashew nuts, walnuts, pistachios, almonds and peanuts are all used. On fast days, when usual meals are abstained from, nuts may be eaten as a substantial meal in themselves.

Other sweets are made of rice (or vermicelli) and milk, or rice and coconut milk – though they are generally eaten as afternoon snacks, they make excellent desserts. Vermicelli, made of durum wheat and semolina, familiar from Italian cooking to many in the West, forms the basis of several sweet dishes, from the everyday sweet vermicelli to the exotic *payasam* – with its delicious combination of sago and vermicelli, raisins, cardamom, sugar and nuts.

Jaggery, palmyra sugar, is used rather than cane sugar, and dark brown sugar makes the best substitute (white sugar can also be used). Coconuts are in plentiful supply in Madras, and are used in many sweet dishes throughout the year, while cardamom adds flavor to many sweet dishes.

Barfi pista

2¼ cups whole milk

4 tablespoons each: unsalted shelled pistachio nuts, roasted flaked almonds and unsalted cashew nuts

or ¾ cup of any one variety

4 tablespoons light brown sugar

½ cup water

1 teaspoon rose-water

2 drops green food coloring

This favorite sweetmeat is generally given as a gift upon the birth of a daughter – having sons myself, I would like to dedicate this recipe to my niece, who shares my birthday.

1. Place the milk in a heavy-based saucepan; over very low heat reduce it to one-sixth of its original volume, stirring occasionally – this will take up to an hour.

2. Roast the nuts; crush them and set aside.

3. Combine the sugar and water. Heat to 210°F to make a thick syrup. Cover and keep warm.

4. Add to the reduced milk the syrup and nuts, coloring and rose water. Stir until the mixture pulls away from the sides of the pan and holds together.

5. Press the mixture in a greased tray. Cut into squares when cool.

Jalebis

1 cup gram [chickpea] flour or self-rising flour

¼ cup rice flour

¾ cup coarse semolina (see Glossary)

pinch of salt

2 tablespoons butter or ghee

2 tablespoons plain whole milk yogurt

1 ounce compressed yeast

½ cup tepid water

a pinch of saffron strands

pastry bag with ¼-inch plain nozzle

chopped roasted almonds (optional)

confectioner's sugar (optional)

Jalebis are a deliciously light, orange-colored spiral sweetmeat that is either eaten hot with syrup as a dessert or cold and sprinkled with confectioner's sugar as a snack during the day.

The batter is piped straight into hot oil. (It may be useful to have a "sous-chef" the first time you make these, as the procedure is rather fiddly.)

◆ The batter needs to stand overnight.

1. Sift the gram or self-rising flour and the rice flour into a mixing bowl (preferably of an electric mixer). Add the semolina and salt. Melt the butter or ghee and add to the flour. Mix in the yogurt, melted butter, yeast, and ½ cup of water, and beat until the batter reaches the consistency of thick cream (add extra water if required). Cover and leave overnight in a refrigerator to ferment.

2. Make the syrup, if using (see next page).

3. Infuse the saffron strands in 2 teaspoons of water for 5 minutes, then add the liquid and strands to the batter.

4. Prepare a pastry bag for use. Heat a few inches of oil in a wok or deep fryer over medium heat. Fill the pastry bag with some batter. Drop half a teaspoon of the batter into the oil to test the temperature – it should sizzle but not go dark brown instantly. Adjust the temperature if necessary. Then pipe a few figure eights or spirals of batter into the hot oil. The batter will set and turn pale gold and crisp. Quickly remove from the oil and drain on paper towel.

5. Immerse the warm jalebis in the warm syrup for a minute, then remove.

6. Continue until all the mixture is used.

7. Serve jalebis warm, in the remaining syrup, sprinkled with chopped roasted almonds. If serving cold, simply sprinkle with confectioner's sugar. They will keep for a while in an airtight jar.

for the syrup:

2 whole cloves

2 cardamom pods

⅔ cup dark brown sugar

1 cup water

1 tablespoon freshly squeezed lime juice

SYRUP

1. Crush the cloves in a mortar and pestle.

2. Remove the seeds from the cardamom pods. Discard the pods and crush the seeds.

3. Heat the water in a pan and dissolve the sugar in it. Add the crushed cloves and cardamom seeds, and the lime juice. Raise the heat. Boil until the syrup is slightly caramelized (190°F). Remove from the heat.

Gulab jamus

½ cup dried whole milk (see Glossary)

⅔ cup ground almonds

1 tablespoon all-purpose flour

1 tablespoon baking powder

8–10 tablespoons fresh milk

2 cups dark brown sugar

4 cups water

¼ cup rose water

ghee

Sweetmeats such as gulab jamus *can be served as desserts. They are made with very basic and simple ingredients – milk, flour and ground almonds – and served in a light syrup, either hot or cold. Gulab jamus are eaten all over India. Bear in mind that they are very rich and are best eaten in small quantities.*

1. Sift together the milk powder, ground almonds, all-purpose flour and baking powder.

2. Add enough milk and mix well to form a soft dough. Set aside for an hour, covered with a dish cloth.

3. Meanwhile make a syrup by boiling the sugar with the water and rose water until the syrup thickens (190°F).

4. Form the dough into walnut-sized balls. Deep fry them a few at a time in hot ghee over medium heat until golden brown – the gulab jamus cook extremely quickly and burn easily, so you will need to stay by them the whole time; make up all the dough into balls before frying starts.

5. Drain the gulab jamus on paper towel. Put them in hot syrup and allow them to soak for half an hour before serving.

Kulfi

2 eggs

¼ cup blanched pistachio nuts or almonds

2¼ cups whole milk

¼ cup sugar

¼ cup heavy cream

1 teaspoon rose water

3 drops of green food coloring (optional)

To serve: wafer biscuits

This is the well-known and popular ice-cream dessert eaten through-out India. I would like to dedicate this recipe to my students in my classes.

1. Separate the eggs. Lightly beat the yolks, reserve the whites.

2. Quarter, or roughly chop, the nuts.

3. In a large, heavy-based saucepan heat the milk over a low flame until some of the liquid has evaporated (do not allow to boil). Add the sugar and cream, stirring until sugar dissolves. Reduce the heat. Add the rose water, nuts, egg yolks and coloring (optional).

4. Continue simmering for an additional 5 minutes, beating the mixture with a wooden spoon.

5. Bring to the boil. Pour the mixture into a metal tray. Allow to cool, then freeze until three-quarters set.

6. Whisk the egg whites in a large bowl until stiff. Remove the tray from freezer and fold the contents into the egg whites. Pour the mixture back into the tray. Freeze until set. Serve with wafer biscuits or other light, not-too-sweet cookies.

Curd cheese (or ricotta) quenelles in syrup

RASAGULLAS

MAKES 8 (ALLOW 2 PER PERSON)

1 cup curd cheese (quark) or ricotta

⅓ cup coarse semolina (see Glossary)

1 teaspoon baking powder

8 almonds

1 cup plus 2 tablespoons water

½ cup sugar [use superfine sugar if available]

1 teaspoon rose water

Tamilian men shower their wives with boxes of sweetmeats on birthdays and wedding anniversaries. Women give rasagullas *to their husbands when a son is born, and they distribute them to family members and friends. Curd cheese (quark) and ricotta are suitable for rasagullas.*

1. Mix the cheese with the semolina and baking powder to form a pliable mixture. Knead into a soft dough. Form into walnut-size balls. Push an almond into the center of each ball, and close the dough over the opening. Cover and set aside. Have four dessert dishes ready for use.

2. In another large pan heat the water and dissolve the sugar in it. Raise the heat and boil the syrup for 10 minutes (170°F), until it is pale gold in color. Transfer a third of the syrup into a heatproof container, stir in the rose water and allow to cool. Keep the remaining syrup simmering over low heat.

3. Lower the rasagullas into the simmering syrup, and poach until they increase in size and sink (around 10–15 minutes). Remove from the syrup with a slotted spoon and place two in each dessert dish. Spoon a little of the cooled syrup over the rasagullas and serve.

Payasam

The special taste of payasam comes from the combination of vermicelli, sago, cardamom, raisins, milk and sugar. It is rich, and a little goes a long way. Payasam is the classic dessert at weddings and other special functions.

1 cup water

1 cup whole sago (see Glossary)

¼ cup shelled, unsalted cashew nuts

4 cardamom pods

½ pound vermicelli

½ teaspoon salt, or to taste

2¼ cups milk

1⅓ cups light brown sugar

2 tablespoons raisins

2 tablespoons ground almonds

1. Boil the water and add sago to it. Keep stirring, so that it does not stick to the pan, until the whole sago becomes translucent. Lower the heat and simmer for 10–15 minutes.

2. Fry the cashew nuts and cardamom pods in ghee.

3. Break the vermicelli into lengths of about ½ inch. Add to the cashew nuts and cardamoms and fry until brown.

4. Add the fried ingredients to the simmering sago with the salt, milk, sugar and raisins.

5. When the mixture thickens slightly add the ground almonds.

6. Stir for a minute or two. Serve hot.

Green gram payasam

PACHAI PARPU PAYASAM

This payasam makes use of another legume found in Madras, green grams (moong dhall) [in the U.S., known as mung beans]. Green gram payasam, cooked in rich coconut milk and sugar, is appealing to schoolchildren on cold wet days when they come home hungry.

♦ The grams need to be soaked for 4–5 hours or overnight.

½ cup green grams (moong dhall)

1 cardamom pod

¼ cup thick coconut milk (see Glossary)

¼ cup milk

¼ cup sugar

1. Soak the green grams overnight. Simmer in plenty of water over a low heat until soft (15–20 minutes).

2. Split open the cardamom to release the seeds and discard the pod.

3. When the green grams are soft, drain if necessary and add the coconut milk, fresh milk, sugar and cardamom seed. Cook for another 10 minutes. Serve hot.

Pongal

1 cup short-grain rice

½ cup green grams (moong dhall) [known in U.S. as mung beans]

¼ cup shelled, unsalted cashew nuts

2 or 3 cardamom pods

2 tablespoons ghee

3 cups water

pinch of salt

½ cup brown sugar

½ cup grated coconut

2 tablespoons raisins

Pongal is the harvest festival held in January. It is also a sweet rice dish, served for breakfast or as a dessert on the day of the harvest festival from which it takes its name. Children love the taste, and anyone who enjoys rice pudding will like this.

1. Wash rice and green grams together. Drain and leave aside. Chop the cashew nuts. Deseed the cardamom pods and throw the pods away.

2. In the ghee fry the drained rice and green grams. Add water and bring to the boil. Then add a pinch of salt, sugar, grated coconut and cardamom seeds and stir gently. Lower the heat and cook until the rice and green grams are cooked.

3. Fry the cashew nuts. Just before the rice is cooked add the cashew nuts and the raisins. Serve hot.

Sweet vermicelli

PREMALAR

¼ pound vermicelli

ghee

2 tablespoons shelled, unsalted cashew nuts

¼ cup granulated brown sugar

¼ teaspoon salt (or to taste)

1 cup milk

Milk and its products are important to Tamilians as they are considered pure. This milk pudding is easy to prepare and is always a favorite.

1. Break up the vermicelli into lengths of around ¼ inch. Fry in 1 tablespoon of ghee until brown. Remove and set aside.

2. Fry the cashew nuts in the ghee until brown. Add the vermicelli with the sugar, salt and milk.

3. Simmer until the vermicelli is soft and the mixture has the consistency of a creamy sauce. Serve hot.

Ponni

⅓ cup long-grain rice

3 tablespoons blanched almonds

5 cups milk

¾ cup light brown sugar

4 cardamom pods

¼ cup golden raisins

pinch of salt

1 teaspoon rose water

12 tangerine segments

Ponni rice – long-grain rice cooked with milk, sugar, nuts and raisins – can be either served as a hot dessert or added to peeled segments of oranges and chilled to make a cold dessert for parties. It is a great favorite among Tamilians.

1. Wash and soak the rice in water for 30 minutes. Drain. Meanwhile chop the blanched almonds. Pour the milk into a heavy-based saucepan and add the rice. Bring to the boil and, stirring constantly, cook until the rice is almost soft and a creamy consistency is reached.

2. Then add the sugar and keep stirring until it dissolves. Next add the cardamom pods, chopped almonds, raisins, a pinch of salt and the rose water. Keep cooking until a nice consistency is reached. Remove and serve hot immediately or allow to cool completely.

3. If serving cold, peel the tangerine segments and remove their seeds. Place in individual bowls and add the cooled rice mixture. Chill well before serving.

FACING PAGE: *Ponni, gulab jamus (p. 141) and jalebis (140)*

Mandavalli dessert

¼ cup finely grated mild cheddar cheese

1 5-ounce can evaporated milk

2 tablespoons raisins

3 tablespoons roasted slivered almonds

3 tablespoons shelled unsalted pistachio nuts

pinch nutmeg

2 cardamom pods

1–2 saffron strands

In my family, there is a tradition that someone from each generation creates his or her own special dish. I chose to make a sweet dish. Like all Tamilians, I believe life has many sweet moments and this is one of them! This dessert is filled with the milk of human kindness, the richness of fruit and nuts, and a taste of spice. It is extremely simple to make and tastes absolutely wonderful.

1. Mix the grated cheese together with the other ingredients and whisk lightly. Place in the freezer for 2–3 hours. Remove from the freezer half an hour before serving.

Mysore pakh

½ cup water

1 cup sugar

1 cup gram flour

½ pound (2 sticks) unsalted butter

½ teaspoon grated nutmeg

This is a creamy fudge with a slight taste of nutmeg. As its name suggests, this recipe originally came from Mysore, which at one time was a part of the state of Madras. It is still a favorite with Tamilians today. As with any fudge, it can be kept for some time.

1. Heat the water in a large pan and dissolve the sugar in it. Raise the heat and boil until it is the color of light honey (190°F). Remove from the heat and set aside.

2. Sift the gram flour. Melt half the butter in a heavy-based saucepan over low heat, gradually add the gram flour and fry, stirring constantly, for 3 minutes. Then gradually stir in the syrup until it is absorbed.

3. Next add the remaining butter, a tablespoonful at a time. Stir the mixture before adding the next tablespoonful. Cook, stirring frequently, until the mixture pulls away from the sides of the pan and the butter oozes out. Remove from the heat.

4. Spread the mixture into a greased tray (about 8 x 10 inches). Tilt it to one side and drain off any excess butter. Sprinkle with grated nutmeg and cut into squares. Serve warm or cold.

Sweet potato balls

CHAKKRAVALLI KELANGA

2–3 sweet potatoes (1 pound)

2 tablespoons sugar, white or brown

½ cup grated fresh coconut

Trays of specially prepared sweetmeats are exchanged between friends and neighbors during religious festivals, particularly at Duvali and Christmas. This special snack is given to children at this time, since this is the only time when sweet potatoes are available. The soft mashed sweet potatoes are rolled in fresh grated coconut and sugar, and are absolutely delicious!

1. Wash the sweet potatoes thoroughly. Boil them in water until tender, then remove them from the water, remove the skins and mash the potatoes.

2. Mix the sugar and fresh grated coconut. Form the potato into balls, roll them in the coconut mixture and serve them hot or cold.

Casari

6 tablespoons brown or white sugar

1 cup hot water

a few strands of saffron

2 cardamom pods

6 tablespoons ghee

½ pound coarse semolina (see Glossary)

¼ cup cashew nuts

½ cup milk

¼ cup golden raisins

3 tablespoons whole almonds

salt to taste

Casari is a golden-yellow sweet made of milk, sugar, cashew nuts and cardamom, and has always been a firm favorite. Casari is always eaten on the special day each year when Tamil women eat only cold food and pray for the well-being of their children.

1. Combine the sugar and hot water in a pan over low heat, stirring, until the syrup takes on a golden color (170°F). Remove from the heat and leave aside.

2. Soak the saffron strands in 1 teaspoon of hot water. Open the cardamoms and discard the pods.

3. Fry the semolina in ghee until brown. Remove and set aside. Fry the cashew nuts in the same ghee until browned, return the semolina to the pan. Add the syrup, milk, cardamom seeds, raisins and softened saffron strands. Cook, stirring, over low heat until the mixture thickens, then spread in a buttered dish; decorate it with the almonds. Allow to cool for half an hour, then cut into squares.

Cashew or chestnut candy

VEDANAYAGAM MUTTAI

2 cardamom pods

2 cups cashew nuts or chestnuts

¾ cup hot water

½ cup sugar

2 teaspoons rose water

¼ pound (1 stick) butter plus enough to grease the baking sheet

Cashew nuts, brought to Madras by the Portuguese, are sweet with a milky taste. Ground, they are made into a candy which is eaten at the celebration for a baby's first tooth. Chestnuts are even sweeter, and make a nice brown candy for Christmas and Duvali (New Year). This is dedicated to all my friends.

1. Open the cardamoms, and discard the pods.

2. Peel the chestnuts, if using. Roast the chestnuts or cashew nuts in a hot oven or heavy frying-pan until golden brown, then chop very finely or grind coarsely in a food processor.

3. Heat ⅓ cup of water in a heavy saucepan. Dissolve the sugar in it. Stirring well, add the rose water, butter and cardamom seeds and continue to boil to a thick syrup (210°F). Remove the pan from the heat.

4. Stir the nuts into the thick syrup. Stir until the mixture holds together and starts to come away from the sides of the pan.

5. Place the mixture in a greased baking sheet. Allow to cool, then cut into squares. Serve warm or cold.

DRINKS

Sweet yogurt shake

MAJJIKA

½ cup plain yogurt

1½ cups cold water

2–3 tablespoons sugar [use superfine sugar if available]

1 teaspoon rose water

Children sometimes add sugar and fruit to yogurt and have it as a cooling snack in the summer. Here, it makes a deliciously cool drink.

1. Place all ingredients in a blender and blend at high speed until frothy. Remove and chill. Serve when required.

Spiced buttermilk

MORRU

1 cup plain yogurt

2 cups water

2 teaspoons grapeseed oil

½ teaspoon cumin seeds

asafetida (piece the size of a black peppercorn)

a sprinkling of turmeric

salt to taste

two cilantro or neem leaves

A jug of buttermilk is often drunk at the end of a Tamilian meal, either spiced or simply chilled. It is an ideal accompaniment to spicy food or on hot summer days. Traditionally, butter is made from yogurt (curds) rather than fresh milk. Butter is made by combining curds and water, then churning them in an earthenware pot, using a special ridged stick until the solids turn to butter. The remaining buttermilk is then spiced, and drunk at mealtimes. This buttermilk is simply made by whisking the yogurt and water, then adding the spices.

1. Dilute the yogurt with the water and mix well.

2. Heat the oil in a saucepan and add the cumin seeds. When they pop add the asafoetida, turmeric, salt and cilantro or neem leaves, and cook for about a minute or two. Pour the mixture into the buttermilk. Chill before serving.

Fresh lime juice

RAGA

1 teaspoon sugar [use superfine sugar if available]

hot water

1 lime

¾ glass of cold water

In summer in Madras lime juice is often sold from mobile carts to passers-by. It is a very refreshing thirst-quencher, the Indian version of lemonade. The limes used in Madras are almost yellow, and quite sweet. Add more sugar if the limes you use seem sour.

1. Place the sugar in a glass. Add 1 teaspoon of hot water to dissolve the sugar.

2. Squeeze the lime, and add the juice to the syrup in the glass. Top up the glass with cold water, and serve.

Spiced tea

CHAR MASALA

2 whole cloves

3 green cardamom pods

6 cups water

1 teaspoon Nilgiri (or Darjeeling) tea

sugar to taste

Spiced tea is an acquired taste but a soothing drink. It must be drunk very hot. I would like to dedicate this recipe to my husband Bob, who gave me my first English cup of tea and taught me how to make tea in the English way. (Tea from the Nilgiris is available in the United States from specialty suppliers [see source list on page 158] – it has a delicate and slightly perfumed flavor.)

1. Grind the cloves and cardamoms together in a mortar and pestle.

2. Place the water in a pan. Rub the tea leaves with the tips of your fingers to help release the aroma.

3. Add them to 6 cups water and bring to the boil. Then add the ground spices and sugar to taste.

4. Cover and boil for a few seconds. Remove and serve very hot.

Scented chilled tea

CHAYA KADOHI

6 cups water

1 teaspoon Nilgiri (or Darjeeling) tea

sugar to taste

1 teaspoon rose water

2–3 fresh lovage leaves

You may prefer this refreshing but gentler recipe made with rose water and lovage leaves.

1. Place the water in a pan. Rub the tea leaves with the tips of your fingers to help release the aroma.

2. Add them to the water and bring to the boil. Boil for 2 minutes, then add sugar to taste and the rose water.

3. Cover and boil for a few seconds. Allow to cool, then chill. Add the lovage leaves before serving.

GLOSSARY OF SPICES
AND OTHER INGREDIENTS

ANISEED was brought to India from Persia during the Moghul period. The seeds are white and oval in shape, and have a distinctive, sweetish and very aromatic flavor

ASAFETIDA is the solidified sap of the *Ferula foetida* plant. It is very strongly flavored (reminiscent of onion or truffle) and should be used in small quantities, in conjunction with onion and garlic. It is sold in three forms: "tears" (drops of hardened resin, flattened), "mass" and powder (often mixed with yellow coloring). When asafetida is called for in these recipes, I have assumed the use of the mass, usually rolled to form a ball the size of a black peppercorn.

ATTA flour is also sold as chappati flour, or as *godimai*. It is an unrefined, whole grain flour, yet very finely ground, and is easily available from Indian stores. Whole wheat flour is not a good substitute as it contains more of the grain and is much coarser in texture than atta.

BANANA LEAVES are used as wrappings for food and as disposable plates in restaurants and at large functions. They are also used to wrap fish before it is baked or barbecued, and impart a delicious flavor to it. It is hard to obtain banana leaves in the West, especially in small quantities. Aluminum foil may be substituted.

BESAN FLOUR, see GRAM FLOUR

BITTER GOURD (KARELI) is bright green, about 5 or 6 inches long and has a knobbly skin. The inside is white or orange with small seeds, which are also edible. As the name implies, the vegetable is bitter.

BLACK GRAMS, see DHALL, URAD

BLACK MUSTARD SEEDS, see MUSTARD SEEDS

CARDAMOM is a member of the ginger family. The pods contain black seeds. Cardamom pods are gathered from wild plants native to the moist forests of south India. They have a warm, slightly pungent flavor. There are two varieties, white bleached ones and the more popular green, unbleached cardamom. In some recipes, only the cardamom seed is used, and the empty pods discarded.

CHANNA DHALL, see DHALL

CHILI is like the goddess Kali, both a creator and destroyer. Used well it gives a pleasant flavor, but misused it can cause some pain! The heat of chilies is considered in India as purifying. The quantity of chili should always be modified to suit personal taste.

Chilies are not native to Asia – they were brought from South America by the Portuguese, and were swiftly adopted in India, as they are easy to grow and more fiery than black pepper. Chilies come in many shapes and sizes, and are green or red. Red chilies are often dried, and dried red chilies can be ground to a powder.

FRESH CHILIES should always be plump and shiny – as a general rule, the smaller the chili, the more fiery it is. Green ones are used fresh in vegetable, fish and meat dishes. Red chilies are sweeter than green, as they have ripened. Generally fresh chilies need to be slit open, their seeds carefully scraped out with a knife, then to be sliced extremely finely before use. Do take care, as chili juice is a strong irritant. Hands need to be washed immediately after preparing chilies, before inadvertently touching the eyes, for example.

DRIED RED CHILIES give their own special flavor when cooked in hot oil.

CHILI POWDER should not be kept too long, and should always be cooked thoroughly, not added at the end of cooking. It should be fried over low heat, otherwise it can give a bitter flavor. When buying chili powder, take care that it is 100% chili (some brands, intended for Mexican cooking, add other spices to make a chili mix – if in doubt, choose cayenne powder).

CILANTRO, see CORIANDER leaves

CINNAMON is one of the most important Indian spices, and native to the Malabar coast. It consists of sticks of the inner bark of branches, found beneath the outer layer of corklike bark of certain trees. It has a warm, agreeable taste and is used in sweet and savory dishes. These recipes generally specify the length of cinnamon stick required, and the piece is generally cooked whole. It can easily be ground in a coffee grinder, if ground cinnamon is called for.

COCONUT. The white coconut flesh is grated and sometimes used in vegetables dishes, or to make the famous coconut chutney that accompanies dosais, idlis and other savories. The liquid in the middle is referred to as coconut water. COCONUT MILK is completely different – it is prepared by infusing grated coconut in hot water, then squeezing out the milky liquid formed (see box).

When buying a coconut, always check for cracks and mold. There should be plenty of liquid inside.

Coconuts are split into halves easily with the claw of a hammer. Modern Tamilians use a hand grater or scraper, or a food processor. Pry off the outer edge with a sharp knife and peel the brown skin with a vegetable peeler. Cut into small pieces and process to a pulp in a food processor. If using a food processor with a grating plate, there is no need to remove the brown skin – place the piece of coconut with the skin facing upward and stop grating once the flesh has gone through (remove the skin before grating the next piece, of course). It doesn't matter if the grated coconut is slightly pulpy. Grated coconut can be frozen and used whenever required.

Tamilians use three thicknesses of coconut milk in cooking. THIN COCONUT MILK is used during cooking, whereas the THICK MILK is stirred in at the end. COCONUT CREAM (this is not to be confused with purchased blocks of cream of coconut) is used in making sweetmeats. The thickness of the milk obtained is dependent on the quantity of water used to infuse the coconut. Coconut milk can also be made using blocks of CREAM OF COCONUT or packets of DRIED COCONUT MILK.

Many recipes call for both thick and thin coconut milk. Generally the coconut flesh is infused twice – the first infusion produces the thick milk, which is put aside, and the second infusion produces the thin milk. However, if the recipe requires no thick milk, thin milk can be made from a smaller quantity of flesh – see box.

CORIANDER leaves (cilantro) are added to many dishes toward the end of cooking, and make an attractive garnish. The leaves from one or two sprigs are generally sufficient. Cilantro is widely available, and can also be grown outdoors in summer.

MAKING COCONUT MILK FROM FRESH COCONUT:

Adjust these quantities to suit each recipe, but keep the proportions the same. A whole fresh coconut usually yields about 3–4 cups grated flesh.

To make ½ cup thick milk:
infuse the grated coconut in ½ cup hot water for 5 minutes. Strain through muslin.

To make 1 cup thin milk:
infuse EITHER the used grated coconut OR 2 cups fresh grated coconut in another 1 cup hot water. Strain through muslin.

MAKING COCONUT MILK FROM DRIED COCONUT MILK:
(refer to manufacturer's instructions)
To make ½ cup thick milk:
place 2 tablespoons powder in a measuring cup and mix in water up to the ½ cup mark.

To make ½ cup thin milk:
place 1 tablespoon powder in a measuring cup and mix in water up to the ½ cup mark.

MAKING COCONUT MILK FROM BLOCK CREAM OF COCONUT:
(refer to manufacturer's instructions)
To make ½ cup thick milk:
place 1¼ ounce chopped block in a measuring cup with water up to the ½ cup mark.

To make ½ cup thin milk:
place ¾ ounce chopped block in a measuring cup with water up to the ½ cup mark.

Coconut cream (for desserts) is made as for thick milk by any of the methods above, but using only half the quantity of water.

CORIANDER seeds, *dhaniya*, are round and beige colored. Where ground coriander is called for, it can easily be prepared from seeds in a coffee grinder.

CUMIN, or *jeera*, seeds are crescent-shaped and have a distinctive heavy, strong aroma and a warm taste reminiscent of caraway.

CURDS, see yogurt

DHALL is the term given to legumes, or grams (split peas and lentils). It also refers to cooked legumes. The Tamilian name for dhall is *parpu*. Here the Hindi names are given first, rather than Tamil ones, as they will be more useful when shopping in Indian import or other specialty stores.

CHANNA DHALL, *channeh*, Bengal gram or split sweated chickpeas are wrinkled and dark brown before they are hulled. Once the skin is removed, the bright orange or yellow pea is sweated. This dhall is high in protein and has a nutty flavor. It may need presoaking to speed the cooking process. It is an essential ingredient for vadais, and is sometimes used in vegetable dishes if urad dhall is not available.

MASOOR DHALL is the name given to red lentils. They are little used in Madras, but can be used if toor dhall is unavailable (see below).

MOONG DHALL is known by the Tamil name *pachai parpu*, or green grams. [Known in the U.S. as mung beans.] These are small, slightly oval-shaped, and bright olive green. Moong dhall is one of the legumes used in sweet dishes. As the skin is fairly tough the dhall needs to be soaked overnight before cooking.

TOOR DHALL, or *toovar dhall* (red grams), is the most-used dhall in Madras. This legume grows on a short plant with yellow flowers, which form pods that generally hold three peas. The characteristic red skin of the dhall is generally removed before sale, and the dhall has a rich, earthy yellow color. The dhall remains whole when cooked and takes 20–30 minutes to soften (cooking time can be reduced by soaking the dhall for an hour before use). Red lentils (*masoor dhall*) can be used as a substitute, though the cooking time will be less and the quantity of water will need to be reduced.

URAD DHALL is known by the Tamil name *ulandu*, or as split black grams, and is a key ingredient in masala dosais, idlis and vadais. Urad dhall is sold with its black husk intact, or with it removed (sometimes called "snow white lentils"). The recipes here require the hulled, white, variety.

URAD DHALL FLOUR, or *ulandu* flour, is used for another savory, bondas.

DRUMSTICKS, or MURANGAIKA, are the pods of a tree native to south India. They are similar to long green beans, but are often a foot long – they are now available in North America in some Indian stores. The flavor is quite close to that of asparagus. Drumsticks need to be trimmed and cut into 2-inch pieces, and most will need to have stringy parts of their skins removed before cooking. The best way to eat drumsticks is by picking up the pieces as if they were asparagus, eating the best bits and discarding anything tough.

EGGPLANTS are available in many varieties in India, and are generally small (around the size of a small pear). When my recipes call for small eggplants, this is the size intended – the large eggplants usually sold in the West are the equivalent of around four small eggplants.

FENUGREEK SEEDS, or METHI, are yellowish brown in color, have a strong aroma and a sweetish and somewhat bitter taste reminiscent of burnt sugar. They are native to southern Europe. The fenugreek seeds turn sweetish when fried in hot oil and are used particularly in fish dishes. Young fenugreek plants, similar in taste to spinach, are grown as potted herbs in Madras by Tamilian women and the small green leaves are used as a vegetable or a garnish. The leaves, when dried, are used as a herb.

GHEE is clarified butter, with all milk solids removed, and is used throughout India. Ghee can be heated to very high temperatures without burning, and in it food can be cooked crisp (food also absorbs less fat at high temperatures).

Ghee is sold in blocks or in cans, and it need not be kept in the refrigerator. At room temperature ghee is easily spooned out.

GINGER is an extremely important ingredient in Tamilian cooking. Quantities are specified by length, for example ½ inch ginger, assuming that it will be cut from a piece around ¾ inch in diameter. (If the piece of root being used is much thicker or thinner, adjust accordingly.)

GRAM FLOUR, or BESAN [known in the U.S. as chick-pea flour], is a yellow flour made from chickpeas. It mixes easily with water to form a batter for deep-fried snacks, such as onion bhajis, and is used in sweetmeats.

GRAMS, see DHALL

JAGGERY resembles brown sugar, and is the crystallized juice of the palmyra palm. Jaggery has a distinct taste and texture, and the nearest substitute is dark brown sugar. However, jaggery is available from Indian grocers, usually in round or cylindrical shapes.

LOVAGE SEEDS, *carom* or *ajwain,* native to southern Europe, have a sweetish, licorice taste.

MASALA has many meanings – it can refer to a spice mixture or to a dish cooked with the mixture. In Madras, a wet masala can be made from crushed and ground onions, ginger, garlic and chilies (such a mixture forms the basis of many of my recipes). A dry masala (spice blend) is sometimes used to coat meat before it is grilled on a barbecue or baked in an oven.

MILK, POWDERED. Some of the recipes for desserts and puddings (*gulab jamus,* for example) call for dried whole milk; most powdered milk on sale is low-fat, or skim milk, which will not work! Dried whole milk (or full-cream powdered milk, as it is known to Indians) is stocked by Indian food stores.

MUSTARD SEEDS. "Black" mustard seeds, not yellow, should be used in these recipes (in fact they are usually brown in color). These seeds are pungent, but when "popped" in hot oil become sweet and nutty. They are a popular ingredient for all vegetable, fish and shrimp dishes.

MUSTARD OIL is used in fish dishes. It is a strong, dark oil extracted from black mustard seeds. This oil has to be heated until it smokes, to remove its bitterness. Mustard oil is available from Indian grocery stores, and there is no substitute for it.

NEEM leaves are also referred to as curry leaves, or *karavapillai.* These leaves, from the *Murraye koenigii* bush, are widely used as a flavoring, especially in south India. They are sold fresh in some Indian stores, usually as sprigs 10–12 inches in length, with leaves resembling small bay leaves. Dried leaves are also available in small packets.

OIL. It is best to use a light oil in these recipes – the oil used in Madras is generally peanut, which is easily available in the West. Alternatives are canola and safflower oil. Sunflower and olive oils are not suitable. Though frying in ghee is considered a ritual, there are no rituals attached to frying in oil.

OKRA (or ladies' fingers) should be plump and crisp when bought (the tips should snap off easily). The vegetable is gluey when cooked for long, but in these recipes it is cooked quickly and should be eaten right away, to prevent the stickiness from developing.

ONIONS. The onions used in Madras are usually red onions. Some recipes call for shallots, which are much sweeter and richer in flavor, and sometimes these are combined with red onions.

The art of making a good dish lies in how well the onions are sautéed in the beginning – for onions are the essential thickening agent in sauces, and the greater the quantity of well sautéed onions, the thicker a sauce will be. When being sautéed for a spicy sauce, onions should be fried before any garlic or ginger are added, to ensure that they soften properly.

PEPPER, BLACK. Black pepper is native to the Malabar coast. It was a very valuable condiment and an important article of trade between Madras and Europe, and was used as a medium of exchange.

PISTACHIOS. In these recipes, pistachios are used for sweets, so unsalted ones should be purchased.

POPPY SEEDS are cultivated in India, and used as a spice. These white or beige seeds are sometimes sold as *kasakasa,* or *khus khus,* and should not be confused with the blue-black variety. (In India, young poppy plants are grown as a potted herb and their leaves sometimes eaten.)

POTATOES are grown all year round in Madras – we have no "old potatoes" stored for winter. Most potatoes are young, pale golden to a rich yellow, and tend to be similar to the waxy varieties available in the United States. Most recipes that call for potatoes will work best with fairly new potatoes.

ROSE WATER. Rose petals are dried and made into rose water, which is available in Indian or Middle Eastern stores and used mainly in sweet dishes. A few drops are sufficient to flavor a dish as it is quite concentrated.

SAFFRON. The purple saffron crocus has been treasured throughout the ages for its golden-colored pungent stigmas used in flavoring and coloring food. Saffron is the most expensive spice in the world today (not surprisingly, as a pound of saffron requires around 75,000 flowers and intensive labor to produce). Saffron should be used sparingly – just a few strands per dish – as its bitter note may otherwise come to the fore. A dye, distilled from saffron in India in ancient times, was used by the followers of Buddha for their robes.

SAGO. Small, white, grains that become translucent when cooked. Sago is an ingredient of *payasam*, a favorite sweet dish.

SEMOLINA is derived from wheat. The semolina called for in Western recipes is usually very fine – the sweets recipes in this book that use semolina require coarse or very coarse grades, which are available from Indian stores.

SERRATED GOURD has a ridged, rough skin, but is tender inside. This pale green vegetable is available from Indian and Chinese supermarkets. To prepare, peel away the hard, ridged parts of the skin, leaving the softer strips intact.

SESAME SEEDS have been cultivated in Asia since antiquity, for their pearly white seeds that are mild and nutty in flavor. The seeds are often roasted before use, to bring out the flavor – the quickest way to do this is in a heavy pan, without oil. Take care, for once the seeds begin to color they can burn very easily – keep stirring and have something ready to tip them into once they take on a golden color.

SPLIT BLACK GRAMS, see DHALL, URAD

SUGAR. A sugarlike substance, jaggery (see under *jaggery*), is often used in Tamilian cooking, though sugar cane is grown in India. White sugar can be used in most dishes, though dark brown sugar (similar to jaggery) will give sweets a nicer color.

TAMARIND. This tree, native to south India, bears lovely yellowish-red flowers and is sometime used as an ornamental tree. The fruit of the tree is a buff-colored pod which has six or eight seeds enclosed in a sweetish acidic brown pulp. The tamarind pulp is infused and the liquid produced is added during cooking. It has a sweetish yet tangy flavor. Pulp is available in two forms: one rather dry and the other (produced in Southeast Asia) is more processed and has less fiber. Weight for weight, either will give the same results. Hot water is added to the pulp and allowed to stand for 5–10 minutes. Then the pulp is stirred, strained and used when needed.

TOOR DHALL or TOOVAR DHALL, see DHALL

TURMERIC, or *baldi*, is a strong aromatic, has a pepperlike aroma and a bitter, warm taste. It is native to south India, and is obtained from a root related to ginger. Turmeric is used in many dishes – it is also used on ceremonial occasions to rub on the skin and act as a perfume. Turmeric contains a powerful pigment, curcumin, which can be hard to remove when spilled on fabric.

URAD DHALL, see DHALL

VERMICELLI is a type of pasta, resembling very fine spaghetti. Indian vermicelli, like the Italian, is made of durum wheat. The Indian variety is darker in color and slightly thinner than the Italian one, but both can be used with equal success.

WATER in Madras tends to stand in water pots before use, so is always at room temperature, almost tepid. This is an important factor to bear in mind when preparing chappati dough – when I first moved to Britain I had to learn to heat the water until tepid (neither hot nor cold to the touch) before working my dough.

YOGURT, or CURDS, has been produced in India throughout history. My recipes call for unsweetened plain yogurt, and some of them (mainly in the Tiffin chapter) specify whole milk yogurt – this is essential for the success of the recipe (in these recipes water is added so that the yogurt is closer in texture to Indian yogurt).

WHERE TO FIND INGREDIENTS

Patel Brothers
18636 South Pioneer Blvd.
Arnesia, CA 90701
(310) 462-2953

Dhanraj
829 Alvarado Street
San Leandro, CA 94577
(510) 357-1406

FLORIDA

Patel Brothers
1930 West 60th Street
Hiatch, FL 33012
(305) 557-5536

Patel Brothers
7409 N. Decatar Road
Orlando, FL 32809
(407) 438-0766

GEORGIA

Patel Brothers
2968 N. Decator Rd., Suite D
Decator, GA 30033
(404) 292-8235

ILLINOIS

Patel Brothers
2542 West Devon Ave.
Chicago, IL 60659
(312) 764-1857/58

Patel Brothers
1631 Oaknon Place
Des Plains, IL 60018
(312) 635-8413

Indian Groceries & Spices
7300 North St. Louis Avenue
Sikoke, IL 60076

J. K. Grocers
2552 West Devon
Chicago, IL 60659
(312) 262-7600

Jai Hind Foods
2658 West Devon Ave.
Chicago, IL 60659
(312) 973-3400, 01

House of Spices, Inc.
2657 West Devon
Chicago, IL 60659
(312) 465-7742

MARYLAND

Patel Brothers
2080 University Blvd.
East Langley Park, MD 20783
(301) 422-1555

Patel Brothers
808-C Hunger Ford Drive
Rockville, MD 30850
(301) 340-8856

India Foods Warehouse
1355 Holton Avenue
Langley Park, MD 20783
(301) 434-2433

MICHIGAN

Patel Brothers
29212 Orchard Lake Road
Farmington Hills, MI 48334
(313) 851-7470

Patel Brothers
37196 Dequindre
Sterling Heights, MI 40877
(313) 795-5120

Patel Brothers
28684 Ford Road
Garden City, MI 48135
(313) 427-4445

MINNESOTA

Patel Brothers
1848 Central Avenue
Minneapolis, MN 55416
(612) 789-8800

MISSISSIPPI

Patel Brothers
1999 Highway 80 West, #10
Jackson, MS 39204
(601) 353-6611

NEW YORK

Patel Brothers
393 South Broadway
Hicksville, NY 10596
(516) 433-9393

Patel Brothers
37–46 74th Street
Jackson Heights, NY 11372
(718) 898-3445

Patel Brothers
42–79C Main Street
Flushing, NY 11355
(718) 321-9847

Patel Brothers
294–01 Hillside Avenue
Bellrose, NY 11426
(718) 470-1356

House of Spices
76–17 Broadway
Jackson Heights, NY 11373

NEW JERSEY

Patel's Cash & Carry
781 Newark Ave.
Jersey City, NJ 07307
(201) 222-7572

Patel Bros. of N.J., Inc.
1361 Oak Tree Road
Iselin (Edison), NJ 08830
(908) 283-4952

Patel Foods
782 Newark Avenue
Jersey City, NJ 07306
(201) 656-1418

OHIO

Patel Brothers
6876 Pearl Road
Middle Birch Hts., OH 44130
(216) 885-4440

Patel Brothers
8138 S. Spring Bay Pike
Miami Burg, Dayton OH
(513) 439-4090

Patel Brothers
7617 Reading Road
Cincinatti, OH 45237
(513) 821-0304

TEXAS

Patel Brothers
5831 Hillcroft
Houston, TX 77036
(713) 784-8332/41

Patel Brothers
318 S. Central Expressway #10
Richardsons, TX 75080
(214) 644-3972

INDEX

A

akkas takali chatanee 118
Andaman erra kutta 68
anna nagar 127
appa odai nethali 79
appams 38
arumainayagam chittaranam 24–5
Athai's uppuma 132

B

bandapur parvakai 50–1
barfi pista 139
bean sprouts and celery with cockles 54
beef: beef vindaloo 104–5
  beef with chilies 105
  masala beef 103
biryani 20–2
bitter gourd, crisp-fried 50–1
black gram flour: bondas 127
Bombay duck with eggplant 80
bondas 127
bread 26–34
  layered wheat bread 31
  Maida's stuffed roti 33–4
  puffed bread 30
  rich white bread 32
  simple flat bread 27–8
broccoli with dried shrimp 52
buttermilk, spiced 151

C

cabbage with mustard seeds 53
carrots with aniseed 60–1
casari 149
cashew candy 150
cauliflower and potatoes 58
cauvery erra poriyal 69

chakkravalli kelanga 149
chappatis 27–8
char masala 152
chaya kadohi 152
chestnut candy 150
cheynaipattinam omelette 126
cheynempet pusnika 55
chicken: barbecued chicken on skewers 93
  chicken kurma 90
  fried spicy chicken 91
  Kotogari chicken 88
  roast marinated chicken 94
  tandoori chicken 92
chickpeas 137
chiddambaram ambat 51
chinne porikari 108
chutneys 114–20
chutta perisa maligai 41
coconut chutney 116
Coimbatore kochholi 60–1
coonor sunthiyam 82
coovum karvada kuttu 80
crab: crab in chilli with tamarind 70
  thambis crabs 71
curd cheese quenelles 143
cutlets 109

D

devanayagam puli kolamba 120
dhall (thuvarai parpu) 62
ding-ding 99
dosais 34–5
drinks 150–2
drumsticks 49
  drumstick sambar 122
duck with coconut 95
dumplings, steamed 39

E

eggplant: chutney 117
  fried small purple eggplant 42
  with tamarind and coconut 120
eggs: Madras omelette 126
  scrambled eggs 126
  spicy eggs 125
elamcha satham 15
elamcha urga 121
enappa chutta vanjaram 78

F

fish and seafood 64–85
  Bombay duck with eggplant in tamarind sauce 80
  fish in banana leaves 78
  fish in tamarind sauce 75
  fried fish 83
  fried spiced fish 81
  steamed fish with mustard 82
French beans: Jiji's beans 48

G

gulab jamus 141

J

jalebis 140–1
Jiji's beans 48

K

kanya kumari sorra 84
karajige tuvai 128–9
karuga chatna 112
karugu bharjanam 94
katrika chatani 117
katrika poriyal 42
kelanga ghashashi 56

kidneys, fried lambs' 111
kirkanna mutta 126
kodaikanal talasani 59
koli kurma 90
Kotogari karagu 88
kozhi shulli 91
kulfi 142
kungamapu satham 17

L

lamb: chops with peppercorns 98
  Grandma's lamb 99
  lamb frikadels 102
  Pondicherry lamb 96–7
  spiced lamb 100
  Tambaram's lamb 97
lentils: spiced cakes 133
  spiced lentils 62
limes: fresh lime juice 151
  lime pickle 121
liver: fried chicken livers 112
  spicy calves' liver 113
  spicy lambs' liver 113
lobsters, masala 72
long beans, fried 47

M

Madras 8–10
Madurai kilanjal 74
Maida's stuffed roti 33–4
majjika 150
Malar's sukkee 61
mambalam mangai praleka 119
Mammalam murungakai 49
Mammalapuram kal erra 72
mandavalli dessert 148
mango chutney 119
masala dosais 36–7
meat and poultry 86–113

meatballs in spicy sauce
110–11
meen moli 76
meenavar isthamana sappata
83
mint chutney 116–17
monkfish in coconut 76
morru 151
muruku 138
mussels, Madurai 74
Mysore pakh 148

N

nagapatinam patani 44
nambar padditaram 103
nandanam bharjita 99
nandanam karajikayi 130–1
nikkama vesavara 102
Nilgiris pachadi 63
nundigrog kelanga 59–60

O

okra: just okra 46
  spiced okra 46–7
omelette, Madras 126
onion bhajis 136

P

pachai parpu payasam 144
padaipai avaraka 43
pakoras 134
palanka keerai usal 52–3
palasani zunaka 53
pancakes: rice 38
  rice and gram 34–5
  stuffed crisp 36–7
panchanaga seekarane 96–7
parathas 31
payasam 144
  green gram 144
peas with lovage seeds 44
peducherri perkankai 50
pepper water 123
pickle, lime 121
pongal 145
ponmund satham 15
ponni 146
poodina 116–17
poonamalee apakava 111
pooris 30

pork: pork with mushrooms
  108
  pork with shallots and
    onion 107
  spiced pork with orange 106
Port Blair isthamana kai kootu
  54
potatoes: fried new 59
  hot and spicy mashed 59–60
  masala 56
premalar 145
pukshan odai marina erra
  kutta 67
pulao: vegetable 23–4
  shrimp 24–5
puli satham 16–17
pulikat nanda 70
pumpkin with fenugreek 55

R

raga 151
rajkumaran masala mutta 125
rameswaram karamana upkari
  52
rani sunthakas 92
rasagullas 143
rassam 123
relish, yogurt 115
rice 12–25
  biryani 20–2
  buttered rice 14
  crunchy rice 16
  decorated rice 15
  rice and gram pancakes
    34–5
  rice with fresh lime 15
  saffron rice 17
  simple rice 14
  tamarind rice 16–17
  tomato rice 19
  yogurt rice 18
royapetta pakoras 134
rungaswamy meen kolomba 75
rungaswamy murangakai
  sambar 122

S

salad, Nilgiris 63
samosas: meat filling 128–9
  vegetable 130–1

satham 14
savories 124–38
semolina and legume snack
  132
serrated gourd with shrimp
  50
shark cutlets 84
shrimp: Andaman shrimp
  curry 68
  fried shrimp 69
  marina shrimp 67
  shrimp pulao 24–5
snow peas with ginger and
  chili 43
spices 10–11
spinach, Madras 52–3
sunthaka bhagayar 106
sweet peppers, charred
  41
sweet potato balls 149
sweets and desserts 139–50

T

takali satham 19
Tambaram chakkalika 97
tambrapane kodava 85
tambraparne arachi kootu 105
tankasi vendakai 46
tayar pachadi 115
tea: scented chilled tea 152
  spiced tea 152
teynempet priyala 100
teynga thoyal 116
thambi odai nanda kuttu 71
thanjavur tuvai 109
thayar satham 18
thekkadi kootu 58
tidli idlis 39
tirunveli vendakai 46–7
tomato chutney 118
trichinnapolli thallitakari 98
trivandrum shutturaichi 113
tuna cutlets, simple 85
tutukori thanduram 93

U

udugamalam satham 16

V

vadais 133

Vasantha's roti 32
vathyar porichar eral 113
vedanayagam mattai 150
vedanayagam shastika 23–4
veddathanai porichar beans
  47
vedduvar vartha 95
vegetables 40–63
  Malar's root vegetables 61
  vegetable pulao 23–4
vegetarianism 10, 43
vellakaran vintheleux 104–5
vellankani masala meena 81
vellankani sundal 137
vellore nethali 83
vengayam pagodas 136
vennai satham 14
vermicelli, sweet 145
villavar kuy 107
virandali urandakari kolomba
  110–11

W

whitebait: crispy spiced 83
  spicy 79

Y

yogurt: sweet yogurt shake
  150
  yogurt relish 115

Z

zucchini in tamarind 51